"I apologize in advance for ~~the fact that this book~~ ok has almost no robo~~ts~~ or exploding ~~~~

I used to spend many hours writing stupid stories, mainly to annoy people, on social networking sites. As I was continually banned from these places, the 27bslash6 website was created as a site that could not be touched by moderators. After posting an article concerning paying for an outstanding chiropractor's bill with a bad drawing of a spider, the website effectively went viral and has enjoyed a relatively large audience since.

The e-mail articles in this collection are verbatim. Having said that, I do, on occasion, change names, unless the person has annoyed me, and I have been known to exaggerate.

—David Thorne

From: Jane Gilles
Date: Wednesday 8 Oct 2008 12.19pm
To: David Thorne
Subject: Overdue account

Dear David,
Our records indicate that your account is overdue by the amount of $233.95. If you have already made this payment please contact us within the next 7 days to confirm payment has been applied to your account and is no longer outstanding.

Yours sincerely, Jane Gilles

From: David Thorne
Date: Wednesday 8 Oct 2008 12.37pm
To: Jane Gilles
Subject: Re: Overdue account

Dear Jane,
I do not have any money so am sending you this drawing I did of a spider instead. I value the drawing at $233.95 so trust that this settles the matter.

Regards, David

THE
INTERNET
IS A
PLAYGROUND

THE
INTERNET
IS A
PLAYGROUND

Irreverent Correspondences
of an Evil Online Genius

DAVID THORNE

JEREMY P. TARCHER/PENGUIN
a member of Penguin Group (USA) Inc.
New York

JEREMY P. TARCHER/PENGUIN
Published by the Penguin Group
Penguin Group (USA) Inc., 375 Hudson Street, New York, New York 10014, USA •
Penguin Group (Canada), 90 Eglinton Avenue East, Suite 700, Toronto, Ontario
M4P 2Y3, Canada (a division of Pearson Penguin Canada Inc.) • Penguin Books Ltd,
80 Strand, London WC2R 0RL, England • Penguin Ireland, 25 St Stephen's Green,
Dublin 2, Ireland (a division of Penguin Books Ltd) • Penguin Group (Australia),
250 Camberwell Road, Camberwell, Victoria 3124, Australia (a division of Pearson
Australia Group Pty Ltd) • Penguin Books India Pvt Ltd, 11 Community Centre,
Panchsheel Park, New Delhi–110 017, India • Penguin Group (NZ), 67 Apollo Drive,
Rosedale, North Shore 0632, New Zealand (a division of Pearson New Zealand Ltd) •
Penguin Books (South Africa) (Pty) Ltd, 24 Sturdee Avenue,
Rosebank, Johannesburg 2196, South Africa

Penguin Books Ltd, Registered Offices: 80 Strand, London WC2R 0RL, England

Most Tarcher/Penguin books are available at special quantity discounts for bulk purchase
for sales promotions, premiums, fund-raising, and educational needs. Special books
or book excerpts also can be created to fit specific needs. For details, write
Penguin Group (USA) Inc. Special Markets, 375 Hudson Street, New York, NY 10014.

Library of Congress Cataloging-in-Publication Data

Thorne, David, date.
    The internet is a playground / David Thorne.
        p.   cm.
    ISBN 978-1-58542-881-6
    1. Internet—Humor.   2. Electronic mail messages—Humor.   3. Practical jokes.
4. Australian wit and humor.   I. Title.
    PN6231.I62T47   2011   2010054343
    818'.607—dc22

Printed in the United States of America
10   9   8   7   6   5   4   3   2   1

BOOK DESIGN BY MEIGHAN CAVANAUGH

For Seb and Holly <3

Free Telescope.
This page, when rolled into a
tube, makes a telescope with
1:1 magnification.

CONTENTS

Introduction

Thank you for purchasing this book. I apologize in advance for the fact that it contains almost no robots or explosions—or exploding robots. My favorite bit of the book is where Richard and Emmeline are shipwrecked on a tropical island and, with neither the guidance nor restrictions of society, emotional feelings and physical changes arise as they reach puberty and fall in love. Later, on page seventy-two, where Richard moves with his mother to a neighborhood in the San Fernando Valley region of Los Angeles, their new apartment's handyman, an eccentric but kindly Okinawan immigrant, teaches Richard not only martial arts but also important life lessons, such as balancing on a boat. If I were being honest, I would admit that the flight commander article is my favorite because I wish I were an astronaut, but as that would make me sound like a geek, I won't.

I used to spend many hours writing stupid stories, mainly to annoy people, on social networking sites. As I was continually banned from these places, the 27b/6 website was created as a forum that could not be touched by moderators. The site in those days got around five hundred hits per week. After posting an article concerning paying for an outstanding chiropractic bill with a bad drawing of a spider, the website effectively went viral and has enjoyed a relatively large audience since.

The name 27b/6 is a vague homage to George Orwell, who wrote the novel *1984* while living in apartment 27b on level 6. Terry Gilliam also used this as a maintenance form name, though with a stroke not a slash, in his dystopian movie *Brazil*.

Also, to answer the question I am most often asked, the e-mail articles in this collection are verbatim. Having said that, I do, on occasion, change names, unless the person has annoyed me. I also sometimes fix spelling errors, as is my prerogative, and bad grammar prior to posting. The characters in the non-e-mail articles are people who have annoyed me, work colleagues, and friends.

Thanks go to my offspring Seb for his part in the fun; Holly, for being my favorite person on the whole planet despite her being American; and Simon, Craig, Leith, Mark, Bill, and Ross for putting up with my juvenile behavior. A big thank you also goes to the people who link to, tweet, repost, and frequent the 27b/6 website. Without them, the hit counters would be only in the double digits.

Regards, David

Overdue account
chiropractors are not real doctors

I read recently of a "qualified" chiropractor who has been using distance healing for quite some time, claiming he can heal you from his living room. There's no need to visit his office—just call or write and he will do the rest. Apparently, he discovered his special chiropractic skill while he was in his car. His foot hurt, and he told it to realign itself. I did not make this up.

From: Jane Gilles
Date: Wednesday 8 Oct 2008 12:19 p.m.
To: David Thorne
Subject: Overdue account

Dear David,

Our records indicate that your account is overdue by the amount of $233.95. If you have already made this payment please contact us within the next 7 days to confirm payment has been applied to your account and is no longer outstanding.

Yours sincerely, Jane Gilles

From: David Thorne
Date: Wednesday 8 Oct 2008 12:37 p.m.
To: Jane Gilles
Subject: Re: Overdue account

Dear Jane,

I do not have any money, so am sending you this drawing I did of a spider instead. I value the drawing at $233.95, so I trust that this settles the matter.

Regards, David

From: Jane Gilles
Date: Thursday 9 Oct 2008 10:07 a.m.
To: David Thorne
Subject: Re: Re: Overdue account

Dear David,

Thank you for contacting us. Unfortunately we are unable to accept drawings as payment and your account remains in arrears of $233.95. Please contact us within the next 7 days to confirm payment has been applied to your account and is no longer outstanding.

Yours sincerely, Jane Gilles

From: David Thorne
Date: Thursday 9 Oct 2008 10:32 a.m.
To: Jane Gilles
Subject: Re: Re: Re: Overdue account

Dear Jane,

Can I have my drawing of a spider back then, please?

Regards, David

From: Jane Gilles
Date: Thursday 9 Oct 2008 11:42 a.m.
To: David Thorne
Subject: Re: Re: Re: Re: Overdue account

Dear David,

You e-mailed the drawing to me. Do you want me to e-mail it back to you?

Yours sincerely, Jane Gilles

From: David Thorne
Date: Thursday 9 Oct 2008 11:56 a.m.
To: Jane Gilles
Subject: Re: Re: Re: Re: Re: Overdue account

Dear Jane,

Yes, please.

Regards, David

From: Jane Gilles
Date: Thursday 9 Oct 2008 12:14 p.m.
To: David Thorne
Subject: Re: Re: Re: Re: Re: Re: Overdue account

Attached <spider.gif>

From: David Thorne
Date: Friday 10 Oct 2008 09:22 a.m.
To: Jane Gilles
Subject: Whose spider is that?

Dear Jane,

Are you sure this drawing of a spider is the one I sent you?
    This spider has only seven legs, and I do not feel I would have made such an elementary mistake when I drew it.

Regards, David

From: Jane Gilles
Date: Friday 10 Oct 2008 11:03 a.m.
To: David Thorne
Subject: Re: Whose spider is that?

Dear David,

Yes it is the same drawing. I copied and pasted it from the e-mail you sent me on the 8th. David your account is still overdue by the amount of $233.95. Please make this payment as soon as possible.

Yours sincerely, Jane Gilles

From: David Thorne
Date: Friday 10 Oct 2008 11:05 a.m.
To: Jane Gilles
Subject: Automated Out of Office Response

Thank you for contacting me.
    I am currently away on leave, traveling through time, and will be returning last week.

Regards, David

From: David Thorne
Date: Friday 10 Oct 2008 11:08 a.m.
To: Jane Gilles
Subject: Re: Re: Whose spider is that?

Hello, I am back and have read through your e-mails and accept that, despite missing a leg, that drawing of a spider may, indeed, be the one I sent you.
    I realize with hindsight that it is possible you rejected the drawing of a

spider due to this obvious limb omission but did not point it out in an effort to avoid hurting my feelings. As such, I am sending you a revised drawing with the correct number of legs as full payment for any amount outstanding.

I trust this will bring the matter to a conclusion.

Regards, David

From: Jane Gilles
Date: Monday 13 Oct 2008 2:51 p.m.
To: David Thorne
Subject: Re: Re: Re: Whose spider is that?

Dear David,

As I have stated, we do not accept drawings in leiu of money for accounts outstanding. We accept checks, bank checks, money orders and cash.

Please make a payment this week to avoid incurring any additional fees.

Yours sincerely, Jane Gilles

From: David Thorne
Date: Monday 13 Oct 2008 3:17 p.m.
To: Jane Gilles
Subject: Re: Re: Re: Re: Whose spider is that?

I understand and will definitely make a payment this week if I remember.
As you have not accepted my second drawing as payment, please return
the drawing to me as soon as possible. It was silly of me to assume I
could provide you with something of completely no value whatsoever,
waste your time, and then attach such a large amount to it.

Regards, David

From: Jane Gilles
Date: Tuesday 14 Oct 2008 11:18 a.m.
To: David Thorne
Subject: Re: Re: Re: Re: Re: Whose spider is that?

Attached <spider2.gif>

It's like Twitter
but we charge people
to use it

I quite like Simon, he is like the school teacher that would pull you aside after class and list, for an hour, every bad aspect of your personality and why you will never get anywhere, while you nod and pretend to listen while thinking about how tight Sally Watts's jeans were that day and wishing you were at home playing *Choplifter* on the family's new Amstrad.

I worked with Simon for a while at a branding agency. He was employed to bring in new clients yet somehow managed to be there for several months without bringing in a single one before leaving to pursue his own projects. The lack of new clients may possibly be attributed to his being too busy writing angry e-mails to other de Masi jones employees, such as "When I worked at Ogilvy in Hong Kong, everyone called me Mr. Edhouse and said that I was doing a great job. Not once did the secretary there call me a wanker or have her grotty old G-strings poking out the top of her fat arse every day, making me feel ill"—which I found much more entertaining than having to do the work that maintaining new clients would have entailed.

From: Simon Edhouse
Date: Monday 16 November 2009 2:19 p.m.
To: David Thorne
Subject: Logo Design

Hello David,

I would like to catch up as I am working on a really exciting project at the moment and need a logo designed. Basically something representing peer to peer networking. I have to have something to show prospective clients this week so would you be able to pull something together in the next few days? I will also need a couple of pie charts done for a 1 page website. If deal goes ahead there will be some good money in it for you.

Simon

From: David Thorne
Date: Monday 16 November 2009 3:52 p.m.
To: Simon Edhouse
Subject: Re: Logo Design

Dear Simon,

Disregarding the fact that you have still not paid me for work I completed earlier this year despite several assertions that you would do so, I would be delighted to spend my free time creating logos and pie charts for you based on further vague promises of future possible payment. Please find attached pie chart as requested and let me know of any changes required.

Regards, David

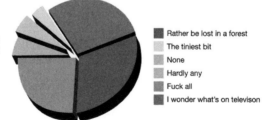

David's enthusiasm for doing free work for Simon

- Rather be lost in a forest
- The tiniest bit
- None
- Hardly any
- Fuck all
- I wonder what's on televison

From: Simon Edhouse
Date: Monday 16 November 2009 4:11 p.m.
To: David Thorne
Subject: Re: Re: Logo Design

Is that supposed to be a fucking joke? I told you the previous projects did not go ahead. I invested a lot more time and energy in those projects than you did. If you put as much energy into the projects as you do being a dickhead you would be a lot more successful.

From: David Thorne
Date: Monday 16 November 2009 5:27 p.m.
To: Simon Edhouse
Subject: Re: Re: Re: Logo Design

Dear Simon,

You are correct and I apologize. Your last project was actually both commercially viable and original. Unfortunately, the part that was commercially viable was not original, and the part that was original was not commercially viable.

I would no doubt find your ideas more "cutting edge" and original if I had traveled forward in time from the 1950s, but as it stands, your ideas for technology-based projects that have already been put into application by other people several years before you thought of them fail to generate the enthusiasm they possibly deserve. Having said that, though, if I had traveled forward in time, my time machine would probably put your peer-to-peer networking technology to shame, because it would have not only commercial viability but also an awesome logo and accompanying pie charts.

Regardless, I have, as requested, attached a logo that represents the peer-to-peer-networking project you are currently working on and how it feels working with you in general.

Regards, David

From: Simon Edhouse
Date: Tuesday 17 November 2009 11:07 a.m.
To: David Thorne
Subject: Re: Re: Re: Re: Logo Design

You just crossed the line. You have no idea about the potential this project has. The technology allows users to network peer to peer, add contacts, share information and is potentially worth many millions of dollars and your short sightedness just cost you any chance of being involved.

From: David Thorne
Date: Tuesday 17 November 2009 1:36 p.m.
To: Simon Edhouse
Subject: Re: Re: Re: Re: Re: Logo Design

Dear Simon,

So you have invented Twitter. Congratulations. This is where that time machine would definitely have come in quite handy.

When I was about twelve, I read that time slows down when approaching the speed of light, so I constructed a time machine by securing my father's portable generator to the back of my mini-bike with rope and attaching the drive belt to the back wheel. Unfortunately, instead of traveling through time and finding myself in the future, I traveled about fifty meters along the footpath at two hundred miles per hour before finding myself in a bush. When asked by the nurse filling out the hospital accident report, "Cause of accident?" I stated, "time travel attempt," but she wrote down "stupidity."

If I did have a working time machine, the first thing I would do is go back four days and tell myself to read the warning on the hair removal cream packaging where it recommends not using on sensitive areas. I would then travel several months back to warn myself against agreeing to do copious amounts of design work for an old man wielding the business-plan equivalent of a retarded child poking itself in the eye with a spoon, before finally traveling back to 1982 and explaining to myself the long-term photographic repercussions of going to the hairdresser and asking for a haircut exactly like Simon Le Bon's the day before a large family gathering.

Regards, David

From: Simon Edhouse
Date: Tuesday 17 November 2009 3:29 p.m.
To: David Thorne
Subject: Re: Re: Re: Re: Re: Re: Logo Design

You really are a fucking idiot and have no idea what you are talking about. The project I am working on will be more successful than twitter within a year. When I sell the project for 40 million dollars I will ignore any e-mails from you begging to be a part of it and will send you a postcard from my yaght. Ciao.

From: David Thorne
Date: Tuesday 17 November 2009 3:58 p.m.
To: Simon Edhouse
Subject: Re: Re: Re: Re: Re: Re: Re: Logo Design

Probability of Simon selling his project for forty million dollars and sending me a postcard from his yacht

None
If using a time machine

From: Simon Edhouse
Date: Tuesday 17 November 2009 4:10 p.m.
To: David Thorne
Subject: Re: Re: Re: Re: Re: Re: Re: Re: Logo Design

Anyone else would be able to see the opportunity I am presenting but not you. You have to be a fucking smart arse about it. All I was asking for was a logo and a few pie charts which would have taken you a few fucking hours.

From: David Thorne
Date: Tuesday 17 November 2009 4:25 p.m.
To: Simon Edhouse
Subject: Re: Re: Re: Re: Re: Re: Re: Re: Re: Logo Design

Dear Simon,

Actually, you were asking me to design a logotype, which would have taken me a few hours—and fifteen years' experience. For free. With pie charts. Usually when people don't ask me to design them a logo, pie charts, or website, I, in return, do not ask them to paint my apartment, drive me to the airport, represent me in court, or whatever it is they do for a living. Unfortunately, though, as your business model consists entirely of "Facebook is cool; I am going to make a website just like that," this non-exchange of free services has no foundation, as you offer nothing of which I won't ask for.

Regards, David

From: Simon Edhouse
Date: Tuesday 17 November 2009 4:43 p.m.
To: David Thorne
Subject: Re: Re: Re: Re: Re: Re: Re: Re: Re: Re: Logo Design

What the fuck is your point? Are you going to do the logo and charts for me or not?

From: David Thorne
Date: Tuesday 17 November 2009 5:02 p.m.
To: Simon Edhouse
Subject: Re: Re: Re: Re: Re: Re: Re: Re: Re: Re: Re: Logo Design

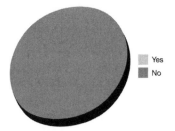

Yes
No

From: Simon Edhouse
Date: Tuesday 17 November 2009 5:13 p.m.
To: David Thorne
Subject: Re: Re: Re: Re: Re: Re: Re: Re: Re: Re: Re: Re: Logo Design

Do not ever e-mail me again.

From: David Thorne
Date: Tuesday 17 November 2009 5:19 p.m.
To: Simon Edhouse
Subject: Re: Re: Re: Re: Re: Re: Re: Re: Re: Re: Re: Re: Re: Logo Design

OK, good luck with your project. If you need anything, let me know.

Regards, David

From: Simon Edhouse
Date: Tuesday 17 November 2009 5:27 p.m.
To: David Thorne
Subject: Re: Re: Re: Re: Re: Re: Re: Re: Re: Re: Re: Re: Re: Logo Design

Get fucked.

Statements
my offspring has made

Sometimes I cannot work out my offspring. One moment he will state something that catches me off guard with its clarity, then the next, come out with something that causes me to think there may have been a mix-up in the hospital.

I was called into his school to speak with the teacher recently. Her statement, "He has a good sense of humor, but he is the only one that gets it," slightly concerned me. But her explanation of why he had received three detentions made me laugh, which is not the reaction she expected:

Detention 1: Raised his hand during math class and asked, "If Kate (a large girl in his class) did not eat for five weeks, would she get skinny or die?"

Detention 2: After teachers had calmed down a very upset child, it was discovered that Seb had told her, "I heard the teachers saying that your parents died today and you are going to have to live at the school."

Detention 3: While the principal was explaining the "no nut policy" due to nut allergies during a school assembly, Seb yelled out, "That's a lot of nuts," after watching the movie *Kung Pow* the night before.

Money
"If I had a million dollars, I would buy a house with big robot legs."

Paying $7.50 for a coffee
"We should open up a shop next to that one, buy their coffees and sell them from our shop for a dollar more."

Our four-door Mazda sedan
"We should paint flames on the side. Girls like cars with flames on the side. You will never get a girlfriend in a car that looks like this."

DVD rental prices
"It makes no sense, this one is four dollars for a whole week and this one is six dollars for one night. It is backward. Someone should tell them."

After being offered a yogurt sample in a supermarket
"She was nice. You should ask her to be your girlfriend before someone else does."

Paying for petrol
"Leaves burn. Why can't we just fill our car up with them? They are free."

On being asked in an elevator what he wants to be when he grows up
"Either a model or a police sniper."

Girls
"You can't trust girls. When I get a girlfriend I am not going to tell her where I live or work."

On being told his mini-bike had been stolen
"I hope they are riding it and the petrol tank blows up and their legs and arms get blown off, and when they are in the hospital, they think, 'I really wish I hadn't stolen that motorbike.'"

The supermarket
"If they made the aisles wider we could drive our car in and grab things through the window and pay on the way out, like at McDonalds."

Regarding my being upset over a breakup
"She was ugly and fat, anyway. I don't even know how you could kiss her."

Explaining the game *Grand Theft Auto 4* to his grandmother
"I don't shoot everybody, just the drug dealers and hookers."

2001: A Space Odyssey
"This movie is so boring. I would rather be staring at the wall and holding my breath for two hours."

Static electricity
"If I am standing on carpet and I get electrocuted, does everybody in the room die apart from me?"

Being told that the park belongs to everybody
"We should buy a fence and make people pay us two dollars to get in."

Relationships
"I am going to have seven girlfriends when I get older so that I can be with a different one every day and then start again on Mondays."

Swimming
"If you swim in the sea, then you should always go swimming with a fat girl because sharks will go for her first."

Shoplifting
"If we went into a shop and I put a stereo on and danced, you could run out with a different stereo while everyone is looking at me."

Cleaning
"It will just get messy again. I like it like this; it shows we have better things to do than cleaning."

Marriage
"If you get married, do you have to let your wife look at your penis?"

Super Powers

"If I could have only one super power it would be to breathe in space."

On having homosexuality explained

"That's gross. Not the bit about girls kissing girls, though, that's pretty good."

School

"I don't understand why I have to go to school at all; the Internet knows more than all the teachers there put together."

Hygiene

"You should never wash your hands; that way, you will have more germs than everything else, and germs won't go on you because there is no room."

Education
should be secondary to discipline

I do not get along all that well with my son's teacher. Since the day she gave him a brochure explaining "the real meaning of Easter," I have had my eye on her. Recently, my offspring took a game called *Tower Defense* to school on his USB drive. As far as games are concerned, it is strategic and positive. At least it's not about stealing autos and shooting hookers. While I understand it was a breach of the rules, I do not feel being banned from using school computers is an appropriate punishment. I do, however, feel that an appropriate punishment for handing out medieval metaphysic propaganda to children would be a good old-fashioned stoning.

From: Margaret Bennett
Date: Friday 22 August 2009 3:40 p.m.
To: David Thorne
Subject: computer room

Hello David

I tried to call you but your phone is off. Just letting you know that Seb bought a flash drive to school yesterday and copied a game onto the school computers which is against the school rules and he has been banned from using the computer room for the rest of the term.

Sincerely, Margaret

From: David Thorne
Date: Monday 24 August 2009 9:16 a.m.
To: Margaret Bennett
Subject: Re: computer room

Dear Maggie,

Thank you for your e-mail. I am not answering my mobile phone at the moment due to a few issues with my landlord and neighbors. I am also experiencing iPhone envy and every second spent using my Nokia is like being trapped in a loveless marriage. Where you stay together for the kids. And the kids all have iPhones. I was not aware that my son taking software to school was in breach of school rules. Although the game is strategic and public domain, not to mention that it was I who copied it and gave it to him, I agree that banning him from access to the computers at school is an appropriate punishment. Especially considering his enthusiasm for the subject. Also, though physical discipline is no longer administered in the public school system, it would probably be appropriate in this instance if nobody is watching. I know from experience that he can take a punch.

Regards, David

From: Margaret Bennett
Date: Tuesday 25 August 2009 10:37 a.m.
To: David Thorne
Subject: Re: Re: computer room

David

We would never strike a student and whether the software is pirated or not is not the issue. He denied having the drive which means he knew he shouldn't have it here then it was found in his bag so I feel the punishment is suitable.

Margaret

From: David Thorne
Date: Tuesday 25 August 2009 11:04 a.m.
To: Margaret Bennett
Subject: Re: Re: Re: computer room

Dear Maggie,

Yes, I agree. Education and access to the tools necessary for such should always come secondary to discipline. When I was young, discipline was an accepted part of each school day. Once, when I colored outside the lines, I was forced to stand in the playground with a sign around my neck that read "non-conformist" while the other children pelted me with rubble from the recently torched school library. Apparently, a copy of *Biggles* had been found behind a filing cabinet.

Another time, because I desperately wanted a *Battlestar Galactica* jacket like Apollo in the television series, using brown house paint from the shed at home, I painted my denim jacket and used Araldite to attach brass door hinges as clasps. Feeling that it was an excellent representation, and despite the oil-based paint still being soaking wet, I wore it to school the next day. Unfortunately, the paint dried while I was sitting in Mrs. Bowman's English class, securing me to the chair. After the school handyman cut me free, I was sent to the principal for damaging school property. My punishment was to scrape wads of chewing gum off the bottom of every chair in the school after hours. It took several weeks, and it was during this lonely time that I created my imaginary friend Mr. Wrigley. During class, when the teacher was not looking, we would pass each other notes regarding the merits of disciplinary action and how one day we would own real *Battlestar Galactica* jackets.

Also, if you happen to see Seb eating anything over the next few weeks, please take the food from him immediately. He forgot to feed his turtle last week, and I feel a month without food will help him understand both the importance of being a responsible pet owner and the effects of malnutrition.

Regards, David

From: Margaret Bennett
Date: Tuesday 25 August 2009 4:10 p.m.
To: David Thorne
Subject: Re: Re: Re: Re: computer room

I hope you are not being serious about the food but I am forwarding your e-mail to the principal as per school policy.

From: David Thorne
Date: Wednesday 26 August 2009 11:18 a.m.
To: Margaret Bennett
Subject: Re: Re: Re: Re: Re: computer room

Dear Maggie,

Rest assured, I would not really withhold nutritional requirements from any child. Except maybe that one that starred in the *Home Alone* movies. I read somewhere that a healthy breakfast helps concentration, and since replacing my usual diet of nicotine with Froot Loops, I have found I am able to move small objects with my mind. Just this morning Seb and I were discussing the importance of good nutrition, which is why, if you check in his school bag, you will find a bag of rice, vegetables, a wok, and a camp stove. The gas bottle can be a little tricky but has instructions printed on the side, so he should be all right. Please remind him to stand well back and cover his face while igniting, as the hose is worn and has developed a small leak.

Also, I am not sure what you are teaching in your classroom, but Seb came home the other week talking about a healthy eating pyramid. I had to explain to him that pyramids are made of stone and therefore not edible, so I would appreciate your not filling his head with these fanciful notions.

Regards, David

From: Margaret Bennett
Date: Wednesday 26 August 2009 2:05 p.m.
To: David Thorne
Subject: Re: Re: Re: Re: Re: Re: computer room

I have no idea what your point is. I will speak to the principal about the ban but you have to understand that only government approved software is allowed on the computers and Seb knew this rule.

Margaret

From: David Thorne
Date: Wednesday 26 August 2009 2:17 p.m.
To: Margaret Bennett
Subject: Re: Re: Re: Re: Re: Re: Re: computer room

Dear Maggie,

I understand the need for conformity. Without a concise set of rules to follow we would probably all have to resort to common sense. Discipline is the key to conformity, and it is important that we learn not to question authority at an early age.

Just this week I found a Sue Townsend novel in Seb's bag that I do not believe is on the school-approved reading list. Do not concern yourself about it making its way to the schoolyard, though, because we attended a community book burning last night. Although one lady tried to ruin the atmosphere with comments regarding Mayan codices and the Alexandrian Libraries, I mentioned to the High Magus that I had overheard her discussing spells to turn the village cow's milk sour, and the mob took care of the rest.

Regards, David

From: Margaret Bennett
Date: Thursday 28 August 2009 11:56 a.m.
To: David Thorne
Subject: Re: Re: Re: Re: Re: Re: Re: Re: computer room

I have spoken to the principal and in this instance we will lift the ban.

Margaret

I wish I had a monkey,
not like this one, though

If a woman had sex with a gorilla, got pregnant, and gave birth, we would be able to see what man's early ancestors really looked like and include actual photographs in scientific volumes dealing with Neanderthal man. Due to the mixing of species, it might not be possible to produce off-spring, or it might be more likely if a man had sex with a female gorilla, but this would be much less fun to watch. Due to father/mother percentage variations, we would probably need about fifty women to do it to get an average. We could also put the babies on an island with hidden cameras to see if they invent the wheel and discover fire. Call it Monkey Island and sell series rights. Another bonus would be enough actors to produce foot-age that would make the opening scenes from *2001: A Space Odyssey* look like a primary school play. I would call mine Manky, as it is a cross between man and monkey; and I would teach him to love.

Obviously, having my own monkey would be fantastic for a whole host of reasons, but as they are quite intelligent yet unable to speak, they have the advantage of learning very quickly through beatings while being unable to tell anyone. The following is a list of the kinds of monkeys that would be good to have. The list is far from complete, as it omits Jet-ski Monkey, Boiling Water Monkey, and *Battlestar Galactica* Monkey but covers the basic best kinds of monkeys.

Disguised Monkey

If I had a monkey, I would borrow my mum's sewing machine and make my monkey a little monkey suit. Then if anyone said, "That's not a real monkey; it's just a monkey suit—I can see the zipper," I could say, "I bet you fifty dollars it is a real monkey." And when they said, "That seems like a reasonable bet. You are on!" my monkey would take off the monkey suit, and they would have to pay me fifty dollars. I would buy drugs with the fifty dollars. For the monkey. So he wouldn't mind spending his life in a monkey suit.

Gambling Monkey

If I had a monkey, I would teach him to count cards like Dustin Hoffman in the movie *Rainman* and then sneak my monkey into the casino. If anyone said, "Hey, a monkey! Whose monkey is that?" I would say, "It's not my monkey."

Hairdressing Monkey

If I had a monkey, I would teach him how to do my hair—using the appropriate amount of product. I would then set the alarm for him to get up half an hour before I do and do my hair while I am still asleep. This would either give me more time in the morning or allow me to spend more time sleeping. I would just waste the extra half hour, anyway, so probably better to sleep; but as I usually don't rock up to work till ten thirty or so, I could try leaving earlier. This would give me more time to write about what I would do if I had a monkey.

Singing Monkey

If I had a monkey, I would teach it to sing Kylie Minogue songs. Then if Kylie passed out on stage again I would be able to save the day by having my monkey finish the concert for her. The concert promoters would probably give me free tickets and promotional gifts. Kylie would be so thankful that she might send me an autographed photo, and I could sell it on eBay for fifty dollars. I would buy drugs with the fifty dollars. Not for the monkey, for me.

Paddling Monkey

If I had a monkey, I would teach it how to use a paddle. The next time I went kayaking I would be able to relax and enjoy the scenery while my monkey navigated the river. The last time I went kayaking, I was listening to my iPod. I fell asleep and got sunburned, and the current took me way up the river before I awoke when the kayak hit a tree branch, and I had to paddle all the way back. Having a paddling monkey would prevent this from ever happening again, so really, it is a water-safety issue and should be encouraged.

Web Monkey

If I had a monkey, I would teach it to download porn for me. This way I could spend my time watching it instead of looking for it. I estimate this would save me one hundred and thirty hours a week. I would obviously require a monkey with similar tastes to mine, but how hard can it be to find a monkey with a penchant for pregnant German women in latex?

Channel Changing Monkey

If I had a monkey, I would teach it how to use all the entertainment equipment. I would save money on batteries for the remote controls by having my monkey change channels for me. With the money I saved on batteries I would buy drugs. I would share the drugs with the monkey while we watched *Black Books* and Stephen Chow movies together.

Surveillance Monkey

If I had a monkey, I would teach it to track down people who annoy me by using their profile photo and Google Maps. Using earpieces to communicate, I would have my monkey conceal himself behind the person typing on Facebook®, and when that person wrote something stupid, I would have my monkey run up and slap them on the back of the head really hard then make a quick escape. Having several monkeys would be more convenient, but I don't have time to train seven monkeys, what with having to do my own hair in the morning.

5 FUN THINGS TO DO WITH A MONKEY

1. Construct and fly box kites
2. EyeToy
3. Run down sand dunes
4. Play Connect 4
5. Dress up

Yellow Shirt Monkey

If I had a monkey, I would name it Brendon. I would shave the monkey, buy it a yellow shirt, and teach it to write inane posts on the Australian wall. Occasionally I would burn the monkey with a cigarette lighter but not to cause enough damage to detract it from its primary goal: impersonating a retard.

Ceramic Monkey

If I had a monkey, I would name it Steve Darls and use it for scientific research. I would then publish my findings in a journal titled "Monkey vs. Electricity." With the proceeds from the sale of this publication, I would buy a potter's wheel and kiln and produce my own range of contemporary, modern statues of monkeys. I could make a cast of my dead monkey and use it to produce to-scale ceramic monkeys. I would design a sticker stating that part of the proceeds go to Greenpeace but would keep all the money for myself. With the money, I would buy drugs and spend my days stoned, listening to music and turning pots.

Hello! My name is Matthew and I have moved into Apartment 3. I m having a house warming party next week on the 14th, if the noise gets to loud that night let me know. Nice to meet you anyhow let me know if you ever need anything.

Cheers Matthew

mobile 04███████

email matthews██████████.au

Dear neighbor,
you are not invited
to my party

A few weeks ago, a guy moved into the apartment across from me. I know little about him apart from the fact that he owns cane furniture; I saw the delivery guys carry it up. I bumped into him on the stairs once, and he said hello, but I cannot be friends with someone that owns cane furniture, so I pretended I had a turtle to feed or something. Last week when I checked my mailbox, I found that my new neighbor had left me a note stating that he was having a party and to let him know if the noise was too loud. The problem I have with the note is not that he was having a party and didn't invite me, it was that he selected a vibrant background of balloons, effectively stating that his party was going to be vibrant and possibly have balloons, and that I couldn't come. If I were writing a note to my neighbors saying that I was going to have a party but none of them could come, I would not add photos of ecstasy tablets, beer, and gratuitous shots of Lucius going down on men to show them what they are missing out on. I would make it clean and simple, possibly even somber, so they didn't think, "You prick."

From: David Thorne
Date: Monday 8 Dec 2008 11:04 a.m.
To: Matthew Smythe
Subject: R.S.V.P.

Dear Matthew,

Thank you for the party invite. At first glance I thought it may be for a child's party—what with it being vibrant and having balloons—but I realize you probably did your best with what little tools were available. I wouldn't miss it for the world. What time would you like me there?

Regards, David

From: Matthew Smythe
Date: Monday 8 Dec 2008 3:48 p.m.
To: David Thorne
Subject: Re: R.S.V.P.

Hi David

Sorry the note was just to let you know that we might be a bit loud that night. The house warming is really just for friends and family but you can drop past for a beer if you like. Cheers Matthew

From: David Thorne
Date: Monday 8 Dec 2008 5:41 p.m.
To: Matthew Smythe
Subject: Re: Re: R.S.V.P.

Thanks Matthew,

Including me in your list of friends and family means a lot. You and I don't tend to have long discussions when we meet in the hallway, and I plan to put a stop to that. Next time we bump into each other I intend to have a very long conversation with you, and I am sure you are looking forward to that as much as I am. I have told my friend Ross that you are having a party, and he is as excited as I am. Do you want us to bring anything or will everything be provided?

Regards, David

From: Matthew Smythe
Date: Tuesday 9 Dec 2008 10:01 a.m.
To: David Thorne
Subject: Re: Re: Re: R.S.V.P.

Hi David

As I said, my housewarming is just for friends and family. There is not a lot of room so cant really have to many people come. Sorry about that mate.

Cheers Matthew

From: David Thorne
Date: Tuesday 9 Dec 2008 2:36 p.m.
To: Matthew Smythe
Subject: Re: Re: Re: Re: R.S.V.P.

Dear Matthew,

I can appreciate that. Our apartments are not very large, are they? I myself like to go for a jog every night to keep fit but fear leaving the house, so I have to jog on the spot, taking very small steps with my arms straight down. I understand the problems of space restrictions all too well. If you would like to store some of your furniture at my place during the party, you are quite welcome to—if we move your cane furniture into my spare room for the night and scatter cushions on the ground, that would provide a lot more seating and create a cozy atmosphere at the same time. I have a mirror ball that you can borrow.

I have told Ross not to invite anyone else due to the space constraints, so it will just be us two and my other friend Simon. When I told Simon that Ross and I were going to a party he became quite angry that I had not invited him as well, so I really didn't have any choice, because he can become quite violent. Sometimes I am afraid to even be in the same room as him. So just me, Ross, and Simon. Simon's girlfriend, Cathy, has a work function on that night but might come along after that if she can get a lift with friends.

Regards, David

From: Matthew Smythe
Date: Tuesday 9 Dec 2008 4:19 p.m.
To: David Thorne
Subject: Re: Re: Re: Re: Re: R.S.V.P.

Wtf? Nobody can come to the houswarming party—it is just for friends and family. I dont even know these people. How do you know I have cane furniture? Are you the guy in apartment 1?

From: David Thorne
Date: Tuesday 9 Dec 2008 6:12 p.m.
To: Matthew Smythe
Subject: Re: Re: Re: Re: Re: Re: R.S.V.P.

Hi Matthew,

I understand it is an exclusive party, and I appreciate your trusting my judgment on who to bring. I just assumed you have cane furniture. Doesn't everybody? Cane is possibly one of the most renewable natural resources we have after plastic, it is not only strong but also lightweight and attractive. Every item in my apartment is made of cane, including my television. It looks like the one from *Gilligan's Island* but is in color, of course. Do you remember that episode where a robot came to the island? That was the best one, in my opinion. I always preferred Mary Anne to Ginger, same with *Flintstones*—I found Betty much more attractive than Wilma, but then I am not really keen on redheads at all. They have freckles all over their body, did you know? It's the ones on their back and shoulders that creep me out the most.

Anyway, Ross rang me today all excited about the party and asked me what the theme is. I told him that I don't think there is a theme; and we discussed it and feel that it should be an eighties-themed party. I have a white suit and projector and am coming as Nik Kershaw. I have made a looping tape of "Wouldn't It Be Good" to play, as I am sure you will agree that this song rocks and has stood the test of time well. I am in the process of redesigning your invites appropriately and will get a few hundred of them printed off later today. I will have to ask you for the money for this because print cartridges for my Epson are pretty expensive. They stopped making this model a month after I bought it, and I have to get the cartridges sent from China. Around $120 should cover it. You can just pop the money in my letterbox if I don't see you before tonight.

Regards, David

From: Matthew Smythe
Date: Wednesday 10 Dec 2008 11:06 p.m.
To: David Thorne
Subject: Re: Re: Re: Re: Re: Re: Re: R.S.V.P.

What the fuck are yout alking about? There is no theme for the party it is just a few friends and family. noone else can come IT IS ONLY FOR MY FRIENDS AND FAMILY do you understand? Do not print anything out because I am not paying for something I dont need and didnt ask you to do! look I am sorry but i am heaps busy and that night is not convenient. Are you in Apatrment1?

From: David Thorne
Date: Thursday 11 Dec 2008 9:15 a.m.
To: Matthew Smythe
Subject: Re: Re: Re: Re: Re: Re: Re: R.S.V.P.

Hello Matthew,

I agree that it is not very convenient and must admit that when I first received your invitation I was perplexed that it was on a Sunday night, but who am I to judge? No, I am in apartment 3B. Our bedroom walls are touching, so when we are sleeping, our heads are only a few feet apart. If I put my ear to the wall I can hear you.

I also agree with you that having a particular theme for your party may not be the best choice. It makes more sense to leave it open as a generic fancy dress party; that way everyone can come dressed in whatever they want. Once, I went to a party in a bear outfit, which worked out well because it was freezing, and I was the only one warm. As it won't be cold the night of your party, I have decided to come as a ninja. I think it would be really good if you dressed as a ninja as well, and we could perform a martial arts display for the other guests. I have real swords and will bring them.

If you need help with your costume, let me know; I have made mine by wrapping a black T-shirt around my face with a hooded jacket and cut finger holes in black socks for the gloves. I do not have any black pants so will spray paint my legs the night of. It is a little hard to breathe in the costume, so I will need you to keep the window open during the party to provide good air circulation. Actually, I just had a thought—how awesome would it be if I arrived *through* the window like a real ninja? We should definitely do that. I just measured the distance between our balconies, and I should be able to jump it. I once leaped across a creek that was more than five meters wide and almost made it.

Also, you mentioned in your invitation that if there was anything I needed, to let you know. My car is going in for a service next week, and I was wondering, seeing as we are good friends now, if it would be OK to borrow yours on that day? I hate catching buses because they are full of poor people who don't own cars.

Regards, David

From: Matthew Smythe
Date: Thursday 11 Dec 2008 3:02 p.m.
To: David Thorne
Subject: Re: Re: Re: Re: Re: Re: Re: Re: Re: R.S.V.P.

WTF? No you cant borrow my car and there is no fucking 3B. I reckon you are that guy from Apartment 1. You are not coming to my house warming and you are not bringing any of your friends. What the fuck is wrong with you??? The only people invited are friends and family I told you that. It is just drinks there is no fucking fancy dress and only people i know are coming! I dont want to be rude but jesus fucking christ man.

From: David Thorne
Date: Sunday 14 Dec 2008 2:04 a.m.
To: Matthew Smythe
Subject: Party

Hello Matthew,

I have been away since Thursday so have not been able to check my e-mail from home. Flying back late today in time for the party and just wanted to say that we are really looking forward to it. Will probably get there around eleven or twelve, just when it starts to liven up. Simon's girlfriend's work function was canceled, so she can make it after all, which is good news. She will probably have a few friends with her, so they will take the minivan. Also, I have arranged a piñata.

Regards, David

Simon's guide
to buying a sofa from IKEA

Hello, my name is Simon, and I love IKEA so much I want to marry it. Can you believe the prices on glass tea light holders? Seventy cents. That is fucking unbelievable. I will get ten.

Here is my simple step-by-step guide to buying a sofa from IKEA. Some people may think that purchasing a sofa would be a simple exercise, but with determination and a little planning, you can ensure that it is a painful process.

Step 1
Ring David at 7:40 a.m. and ask him if he will come to IKEA with you. It is important to ring this early because David will be disoriented and agree to anything.

Step 2
Ring David again at 8:05 a.m. to check that he got up, because getting to IKEA early is imperative. This twenty-five minute interval will ensure that if David did get up he will be in the shower when you call. Ring David again at 9:15 a.m. to inquire where he is and ask him to get you a large latte on the way. If he declines, tell him not to be a selfish prick and remind him of the time you fed his fish while he was away six years ago.

Step 3
When David arrives, inform him that you are taking his car because it is bigger. This is also the time to inform him that you are buying a sofa and

he will need to rent a trailer on the way. Now that David is at your place you can get ready at your leisure. As you just put the clothes you want to wear in the dryer, he will have to wait an hour anyway. Make him useful during this time by having him edit a website you are working on about Australian architecture.

Step 4

On the way to IKEA, complain about David's choice in music. Demand a better selection. Make David pull over and tune his stereo to your iPod's iTrip and play eighties dance tracks, such as "Big in Japan" by Alphaville, loud enough for cars around you to hear. Sing the chorus. If you get the words wrong, explain that's the way they are in another version.

Step 5

When you get to IKEA, do not go straight to the sofa section. Follow the path IKEA has set for you to take, and stop and look at every item. Point out the price and compare each product by cross-referencing it with the IKEA catalogue. Remember to stop at each location and consult the "You are here" diagram before progressing. Inform David every two minutes of your exact location in the store by marking your journey on the IKEA map with your IKEA pencil.

Step 6

At the sofa section, sit on every couch and pretend you are watching television. Make David sit next to you, like a couple. Also, whenever David is more than five meters away, call out questions such as "What is the foam density of that one?" loud enough for those in a thirty-meter radius to hear. Consult with the staff about every couch. Researching sofas on the Internet before you go will enable you to discuss frame warp and fabric weave. Asking about color choices and availability will involve looking through large sample books. Consult David on each swatch.

Step 7

Once you have made your selection, do not leave the store. Purchase a coffee table and shelf unit and tell David that he will help you put them together when you get home. Also purchase lamps, glass tea light holders, cutlery, ice cube trays, cushions, stackable boxes, an ironing board cover, a quilt cover set, and a rug. Make David carry everything, explaining that you need your hands free to write on the IKEA product slip with your IKEA pencil.

Step 8

Before leaving, inform David that you would like to try the famous Swedish Meatballs at the IKEA restaurant. If he states that he will wait in the car, explain that you are shopping together, not one person shopping and the other waiting in the car. Discuss the meatballs on the drive home.

Light fitment broken.

STEVENSON
STRATA MANAGEMENT

D34

OWNER: Z VULICO	INSPECTION DATE: 30.9.09
TENANT: THORNE / DAVID	INSPECTION BY: Peter
PROPERTY ADDRESS:	

	G	A	P	COMMENTS/SUGGESTIONS
ENTRY HALL				
PASSAGES				
LOUNGE ROOM				woodwork requires cleaning including front door
DINING ROOM				tiles grubby.
KITCHEN		✓		Stove burners req cleaning
FAMILY ROOM				
BEDROOM 1		✓		
BEDROOM 2		✓		
BEDROOM 3				
BEDROOM 4				
STUDY				
BATHROOM		✓		shower base grubby, extractor fan filthy.
ENSUITE				
TOILET 1				
TOILET 2				
LAUNDRY				
GARAGE/CARPORT				
SHED/W.SHOP				
PATIO				
POOL				
FRONT GARDEN				Side fence has been replaced
REAR GARDEN				
WATER METER				

GENERAL COMMENTS

Property is not being maintained to a satisfactory condition.
walls, paintwork, tiles all require cleaning.
Apartment smells of smoke : This is a no smoking tenancy agreement

G - GOOD A - AVERAGE P - POOR

Property to be Re-Inspected in two weeks time.

Dear tenant,
you are grubby and smell of smoke

Peter's profile on his company's website declares that Peter, an assistant rental manager, enjoys cricket and coin collecting. And once swam with sharks. I am not a great fan of rental property inspections but they are preferable to rental property inspections without warning. Especially if you are not home at the time. And you haven't cleaned since the Columbus disaster. And you have an adult movie cover left on top of the television in the bedroom. Next to drugs. One of the worst adult movies I have ever seen was called *Debbie Does Dallas,* which featured a lot of scenes with people wearing clothes and talking about things and, because the movie was shot in the seventies, looked as if they were wearing pants made out of hair when they finally did get naked. The worst adult movie I have ever seen was titled *Marge & Me Xmas 94,* which I found inside a secondhand Betamax video recorder I bought for thirty-five dollars. While it contained a lot of nudity, most of it hairless, and very little dialogue apart from Marge complaining continuously about a cramp and, at one point, the gas bill, they were both extremely overweight and well into their sixties, so I could only handle an hour or so before ejecting it in disgust.

From: David Thorne
Date: Wednesday 30 September 2009 6:04 p.m.
To: Peter Williams
Subject: Inspection Report

Dear Peter,

Thank you for the surprise inspection and invitation to participate in the next. I appreciate your underlining the text at the bottom of the page, which I would otherwise have surely mistaken for part of the natural pattern in the paper. I was going to clean the apartment but had so many things on my to-do list that I decided to treat them all equally and draw pictures of sharks instead. I have attached one for your honest appraisal.

Regards, David

From: Peter Williams
Date: Thursday 01 October 2009 9:41 a.m.
To: David Thorne
Subject: Re: Inspection Report

David

I recommed you take this matter more seriously. You were sent notice of the inspection as part of our normal procedure. In addition to the cleaning, the light fitting in the lounge room is broken and the apartment smells of smoke.

Peter

From: David Thorne
Date: Thursday 01 October 2009 10:26 a.m.
To: Peter Williams
Subject: Re: Re: Inspection Report

Dear Peter,

The light fitting was the victim of a toy lightsaber being swung in a space too small to do the same with a cat. I dodged a leaping double-handed overhead attack, and the fitting, being fitted, didn't. I will grab a matching replacement twelve-dollar fitting from IKEA the next time I require a tiny ironing board cover or glass tea light.

The smell you mistook for cigarette smoke was probably just from the fog machine. Each Tuesday I hold a disco in my bedroom with strobe lighting and a special guest. Since my wardrobe door has a large mirror on it, it looks as if someone is dancing with you. I once dressed as a lady, and it was almost exactly what I imagine dancing with a real lady would be like. Unfortunately, I kept worrying about falling, hitting my head, and being found dressed that way, so she left after only a few dances and a brief kiss. You should come one night; it will be a dance spectacular. I imagine you are probably a good dancer, because you are small, and the smallest member of the Rocksteady Crew was definitely the best one.

Regards, David

From: Peter Williams
Date: Thursday 01 October 2009 1:16 p.m.
To: David Thorne
Subject: Re: Re: Re: Inspection Report

David

I do not appreciate being called small and being sent stupid drawings of me being eaten by a shark. The apartment is to be cleaned and reinspected in two weeks time. You cant have a fog machine or anything like that at the apartment in case the smoke damages the walls.

Peter

From: David Thorne
Date: Thursday 01 October 2009 4:02 p.m.
To: Peter Williams
Subject: Re: Re: Re: Re: Inspection Report

Dear Peter,

I apologize for mentioning your smallness. It must be a subject most people you know avoid. Was it the Rocksteady Crew comment or the fact that the shark was actually very small in the picture, making you, in comparison, the size of a very small fish? I have attached a revised version that you can print out, pin to your cubicle wall, look at whenever you are feeling down, and think, "That Volkswagen looks way too small for me to get into. I must be huge."

Regards, David

From: Peter Williams
Date: Thursday 01 October 2009 5:12 p.m.
To: David Thorne
Subject: Re: Re: Re: Re: Re: Inspection Report

David

Do not send me anymore drawings. I am not joking. I am keeping a record of everything you send just so you know. If the apartment is not clean when we reinspect in two weeks time, we will consider terminating the lease as we have also had ongoing noise complaints regarding the premises.

Peter

From: David Thorne
Date: Thursday 01 October 2009 6:27 p.m.
To: Peter Williams
Subject: Re: Re: Re: Re: Re: Re: Inspection Report

Dear Peter,

Yes, I find loud music helps me relax while I clean, because the music distracts me so much that I stop cleaning. Which is relaxing. I will probably get onto it this week, though, as I do not wish to be evicted. I have developed a severe case of agoraphobia, and residing in an apartment where I can reach all four walls while standing in one spot brings me a feeling of security. Also, the daily culling of plague-proportion cockroaches gives me something to do in my spare time. I class the eighteen cans of surface spray I use per week as sporting equipment.

I purchased one of those electronic things that plugs into the wall that is meant to scare cockroaches by sending a pulse through the apartment wiring, but while it has reduced the numbers, it seems some have evolved to feed off the electrical signal, increasing their size. I am using one as a coffee table in the lounge and two smaller ones as side tables in the bedroom. They would probably be susceptible to carbon monoxide poisoning, though, so I will try running a hose pipe from my car exhaust to the apartment, closing the windows and leaving the vehicle running overnight. It is apparently an odorless gas so should not prove an issue for my son's Cub group sleepover.

Also, I read somewhere once that cockroaches can survive a nuclear attack, so I have been collecting the dead ones and intend to glue several thousand to the walls thereby ensuring my survival should Cyberdyne Systems become self-aware between now and when the lease runs out.

Regards, David

From: Peter Williams
Date: Friday 02 October 2009 10:18 a.m.
To: David Thorne
Subject: Re: Re: Re: Re: Re: Re: Re: Inspection Report

I am not going to waste my time reading any more of your stupid nonsense. Clean the property or we will terminate the lease—the choice is yours. Do not e-mail me again unless it is of a serious matter.

Peter

From: David Thorne
Date: Friday 02 October 2009 10:36 a.m.
To: Peter Williams
Subject: Nom nom nom

One thousand characters
posting within limits

Posting in Internet forums can be fun, but there is often a limit of one thousand characters per post, so every story (including punctuation, spaces, introduction, proposal, argument, and punch line) has to be within a small paragraph. Often, I write something rather insensitive to evoke an angry response. When I was just fourteen, I was given the task of drowning kittens by my girlfriend's mother. I filled a large laundry sink with room-temperature water and held the eight kittens under. As each kitten died and sank to the bottom, it turned and rested, "snuggled" to the previous. I put them in a garbage bag and was carrying it out, when the bag moved and I heard a meow. Opening the bag, I found one kitten had survived. So I drowned it again. And that is an exact one thousand.

Sharks

My son wanted scuba gear for his birthday. That's all he wanted. But I am not letting him swim off by himself to be taken for a baby seal by a great white, and I will be fucked if I am going in there with him to be taken for an old skinny seal by a great white. When I explained to him that scuba gear is only for the sea and he, being such a small human, would be taken for a baby seal by a great white, he stated that he would see them coming because of the mask, and added "Speargun" and "Knife" to his birthday list.

Cats

I promised to look after a friend's cat for the week. My place has a glass atrium that goes through two levels; I have put the cat in there with enough food and water to last the week. I am looking forward to the end of the week. It is just sitting there glaring at me; it doesn't do anything else. I can tell it would like to kill me. If I knew I could get a perfect replacement cat, I would kill this one now and replace it Friday afternoon. As we sit here glaring at each other I have already worked out several ways to kill it. The simplest would be to drop heavy items on it from the upstairs bedroom, although I have enough basic engineering knowledge to assume that I could build some form of spear-like projectile device from parts in the downstairs shed. If the atrium were waterproof, the most entertaining would be to flood it with water. It wouldn't have to be that deep, just deeper than the cat is tall. I don't know how long cats can swim, but I doubt it would be for a whole week. If it kept the swimming up for too long I could always try dropping things on it as well. I have read that drowning is one of the most peaceful ways to die, so really it would be a win-win situation for me and the cat, I think.

Tampons

My son's birthday is next week. When he was seven, I told him to draw pictures of what he wanted for his birthday as a visual list. When I inquired as to one image (which I first took to be a box of colored crayons), I deciphered his explanations as it being tampons. In particular, the multicolored brand. His only references to the product were the adverts featuring a girl jumping out of a window onto a tree, which lowered her into a BMW convertible full of friends; an electric green street racing car with black flames; and the ability to do a single-handed handstand star-jump on a dance machine to crowd applause. I bought him a box and figured he would work it out. Yesterday I asked him what he wants for his birthday, and he replied, "not tampons."

Riddick

While watching the movie *The Chronicles of Riddick* with me last night, my offspring stated that he wished Riddick were his dad. When I asked why, he replied that Riddick is good looking, has muscles, and is a good fighter.

I told him that I wished Matthew (his archenemy at school) were my son because he is better at math and has cool hair.

Girls That Have Said No, Part 1

While working at a horse-riding camp several years ago, I spent a good twenty minutes explaining to a group, which consisted of twelve children and their young teacher, the importance of horse safety before walking behind a horse and being kicked in the head. I recall only walking in a zigzag back to the house with the muffled sounds of children screaming in the background before collapsing and waking up in the hospital. While I was there, with a fractured skull, the teacher brought me in a "Get well soon" card signed by all the children, so I asked her out. But she said no.

Superconductors

If you take the temperature of a superconductor down to absolute zero (around -273.1 degrees Celsius), it ignores gravity and floats. This is a scientific fact, and you are welcome to check—google or YouTube it. My nine-year-old son asked why we couldn't freeze a car to -273 degrees and fly in it, and I told him that the car would neutralize gravity, not reverse it, and the weight of the people in it would make it sink. Also, heat rises, so -273 degrees should really sink unless it is in a vacuum, which means we wouldn't be able to breathe or hear the stereo. You would also need to bundle up well.

Girls That Have Said No, Part 2

Around the time I was twelve, my sister had really hot friends staying over. I would dress in ninja gear, wriggle "Saving Private Ryan, beach commando"-style into her bedroom, and listen to their conversations. Some were educational; most were inane. A few months ago, I was standing in a CD store and a girl came up to me and said, "Are you David?" to which I replied, "It depends" (and immediately regretted because I knew that if she asked me, "Depends on what?" I had nothing). The fear must have shown, because she asked, "Depends on what?" and I replied, like a retard, "On whether it is on or off the record—I have been misquoted by you people before." And she looked at me as if I was a retard before telling me that she had been a friend of my sister's and remembered me, and then actually asked, "Are you still annoying?" So I asked her if she still "squeezed her nipples while thinking about kissing Michael Wilson." After a pretty long pause I asked her out. But she said no.

Anhus Street

A street I drive past every day is named Anhus Street and is very distracting. Every few weeks, someone (I am assuming a kid) spray-paints out the "h," making it read "anus," and then a few days later, someone (I am assuming a local elderly resident) paints the "h" back in. If I were boss of the world I would legally change that street name to Anus Street to annoy both of them.

Girls That Have Said No, Part 3

At the local swimming pool canteen, not realizing until afterward that my penis was caught in the elastic of my swimming shorts with the tip sticking out, I purchased a packet of Twisties and a can of Coke before asking out the girl who served me, but she said no.

Parking Spot

A few weeks ago, some guy in a shitty BMW parked in my reserved-and-paid-for parking spot in a small lot. I printed out an A4 (Helvetica Demi Bold 12 pt.) note stating that this was a paid-for parking spot, and not to park there again. A couple of days later he parked there again. I printed out an A3 (Helvetica Black 42 pt.) sign stating "Reserved Parking—Do Not Park Here," and I used spray adhesive (3M®) to mount it on the wall in front of my spot. When I went to park in my spot the next day, he had written in, after "Reserved Parking," the words "For Wankers." About three days later I saw his car parked on the street, so I printed out a poster in A2 (Helvetica

Black 92 pt., reversed) with the word "Fuckhead" and applied it with spray adhesive to his windshield, ensuring (as per instructions) I sprayed both materials to be bonded. The disadvantage, of course, is that I am too scared to park in my spot; but he is also too scared to park there, so I will class this as a draw for the moment and find a new spot.

Dreams

I hate it when people tell me, "I had a weird dream last night . . ." I don't care, it didn't really happen, and it is going to be boring. Just because you dreamed it doesn't make it interesting to anyone. I knew someone who told me a dream, and it went on for about twenty minutes. That is nineteen minutes and sixty seconds longer than I have to care about something that didn't really happen. Another time she was telling me about a dream her auntie had, so not only was I listening to something that didn't really happen; I was listening to something that didn't really happen to someone I didn't even know. I glass over and my mind wanders after hearing the words "I had a weird dream last night," so it is just a waste of everyone's time. The statement she made, "If you cared about me you would be interested in my dreams," I will put down to the fact that she was an idiot and possibly slightly crazy because she owned more than two cats.

My Confession

When I was in year ten, I would wag school to catch the bus into the city. I would hide the contents of my schoolbag and go to a Christian bookstore called the Open Book, covering two levels and a secondhand section in the basement. I would go in with my empty bag, select expensive theological volumes, and fill my bag with several hundred dollars' worth. I would then use the toilets to remove any price tags before going downstairs to the basement, where they would buy my books for half the retail price. I did this twice a week. I figured that if they caught me I would cry and ask for their forgiveness, and as Christians, they would have let me go; but they never caught on. I remember one person buying the entire Amy Grant tape collection, when it had been on the shelves not ten minutes before. I was saving for a motorbike and bought a Suzuki Katana. The Open Book went broke a year later, so it worked out well for everyone.

Girls That Have Said No, Part 4

Around the corner from my place is a 24-hour petrol station thing where I buy what little products I require that don't come in a can (milk) or feed my car. A girl started working there and I thought she was really nice, but she would serve me and not speak or make eye contact. So I asked her if she had a "carfor," and she asked me, "What's a carfor?" to which I replied, "Driving around in when I am not paying ninety-two dollars to feed it," and she laughed in a very strange manner and went back to what looked like counting in binary in her head. After some small talk (which, in hindsight, she may have taken as admonishing her on the poor choice of videos they sold), I asked her out, but she said no.

Toys"R"Us

Having spent over an hour walking through Toys"R"Us considering gift options for my eight-year-old offspring, here is a brief list of things I would buy and play with myself if they came in adult sizes:

Ninja costume
Star Wars® Stormtrooper® costume
Remote controlled AeroHawk® twin-blade helicopter
Blue Power Ranger® costume
Blow-up wading pool with palm tree and slippery dip
Electronic dance mat for PlayStation®
Pink Power Ranger® costume

Girls That Have Said No, Part 5

A lady (age one hundred and ninety) in front of me at the counter at Myers yelled, "My purse!" then looked at me and proclaimed, "You took my purse." So I said, "Yes, I took your purse. I collect them." And she started yelling at me and the department manager came over, and I had to explain that I was not admitting to the theft, I was being sarcastic. Her purse ended up in one of the many bags she was carrying, but she continued to glare at me without so much as an apology. When the girl served me, she apologized, and I asked her, "Why, did you arrange for someone to act like an old crazy woman for me?" and she laughed and said that I was funny, so I asked her out. But she said no.

eBay

I bought a real dinosaur's tooth fossil recently, with an invoice and a note of authenticity, because it is something I have always wanted. There is a quarry a short drive away that my nine-year-old son and I go to and explore sometimes. When we went there last, I suggested we dig for fossils and miraculously "found" the dinosaur tooth (thinking it would be a big deal to him), but he stated, "No, it's just a rock." When I swore I was positive that it was a Saurischian tooth from the Mesozoic era, he replied that I had "made that up" and for me to "throw it away." I cannot prove to him that it is a real dinosaur tooth without divulging the invoice, and he is never seeing that, since I would have to explain why I didn't buy a PlayStation 3 instead of a 70-million-year-old fossil. Occasionally he picks it up and gives me a disdaining look. Also, I bought some NASA mission badges a while back off eBay. He asked me if they had been in space, and I had to admit that they hadn't, and he stated, "Well, that's just weak, then."

Spider-Man 3

I can get over the escaped convict falling into an open air particle accelerator (we have one in the vacant lot next door, and I am always telling my eight-year-old to stop playing near it); I can even get by the space slime landing coincidently meters from Peter and jumping on his bike. . . . What I can't get past is Mary Jane. What a bitch. In the first movie she lets the school bully do her, then she lets the rich guy, then Peter has a turn. In the second movie, she goes through about eighteen different guys before abandoning her big expensive wedding after realizing Peter is Spider-Man. In the third film I think she does about sixty guys and whines a lot about Peter saving lives instead of coming to the theater to watch her crap acting. Why does he put up with her? It makes no sense and is the one glaring discrepancy in an otherwise completely scientifically believable movie.

Wave Patterns

If a rocket was projected as a wave pattern, setting up harmonics such that they reconstitute the original relationship at another point of space/time, any variations could be sorted by a "key" included to ensure the reconstruction was identical. If so, a flight to our nearest star, Alpha Centauri, being only four and a half light years away, would effectively take only 4.5 years to reach. Harmonic travel is impossible, and I am making it up as I go along; but if we did land on new planets, I would hope that there were sexy girl aliens.

"Ribbons" by Sisters of Mercy

Andrew Eldritch used to be too cool for school. I grew my hair for four years to look like him before someone told me I looked ridiculous, more like Edward Scissorhands than him. I first heard the song "Ribbons" almost twenty years ago while doing 160 km/h in a stolen Mercedes down a dark highway on a dark and rainy night. Which would be very cool if it were true, but it was actually while riding a horse and listening to a Walkman on a sunny day. Which is very not cool. I worked at a horse-riding school and had to get up at 5 a.m. every morning, break the ice on top of the horses' water troughs, and feed and groom the horses. Since the riding school catered to school camps, every day I would ride the lead horse on a set path through creeks and hills with five to ten "follower horses" carrying school kids. To make sure the follower horses did nothing but follow, each was fed a blue pill every morning. No matter what the kids did—kick, hit, fall off—the horse would just follow. Because the job was so repetitive, I used to lick the blue pills before giving them to the horses. Apparently, I worked there for more than a year, but I don't remember any of it.

PERMISSION SLIP

Dear Parent/Guardian of _____Seb Thorne_____

On Monday the 22nd of March, classes from year 5 and 6 will be attending a presentation held outside of school grounds at the Mary Richardson Memorial Hall. During the presentation, the true meaning of Easter will be explained in an entertaining and fun filled play performed by members of the Grange Uniting Church youth drama group. Students must have a signed permission slip prior to departure. If you give your child permission to attend this presentation, please sign and return to the school with your child. If you have any questions about the presentation, please call me on ▮▮▮▮▮▮▮▮▮ or send me an email to darryl▮▮▮▮▮▮▮▮▮▮▮▮▮▮▮▮au

Darryl Robinson School Chaplain

☑ I give my child permission

☐ I do not give my child permission

to attend the Mary Richardson Memorial Hall on 22.3.2010 for a class presentation.

_____

Parent / Guardian signature

Darryl
the kind of friend Jesus would have

While preaching is not allowed in Australian public schools, it is apparently fine to replace school counselors with "Christian volunteers," such as Darryl. A few years ago, the government realized that they could hand over school counseling roles to a willing Christian church without having to pay for the privilege. Now, almost half of Australian public schools have a Christian volunteer as a full-time member of the school community, with parents having no direct control of how much their children are exposed to.

Although usually an advocate of people being entitled to their opinions, sexual preferences, and beliefs, I seem to have developed some form of mental glitch that makes me want to punch Darryl's fat head.

From: David Thorne
Date: Wednesday 10 March 2010 7:12 p.m.
To: Darryl Robinson
Subject: Permission Slip

Dear Darryl,

I have received your permission slip featuring what I can only assume is a levitating rabbit about to drop an egg on Jesus.

Thank you for pre-ticking the permission box, because this has saved me not only from having to make a choice but also from having to make my own forty-five-degree downward stroke followed by a 20 percent longer forty-five-degree upward stroke. Without your guidance, I may have mistakenly drawn a picture of a cactus wearing a hat.

As I trust my offspring's ability to separate fact from fantasy, I am happy for him to participate in your indoctrination process, on the proviso that all references to "Jesus" are replaced with the term "Purportedly Magic Jew."

Regards, David

From: Darryl Robinson
Date: Thursday 11 March 2010 9:18 a.m.
To: David Thorne
Subject: Re: Permission Slip

Hello David

The tick in the box already was a mistake I noticed after printing them all. I've seen the play and it's not indoctrinating anyone. It's a fun play performed by a great bunch of kids. You do not have to be religious to enjoy it. You are welcome to attend if you have any concerns.

Darryl Robinson, School Chaplain

From: David Thorne
Date: Thursday 11 March 2010 11:02 a.m.
To: Darryl Robinson
Subject: Re: Re: Permission Slip

Dear Darryl,

Thank you for the kind offer. Being unable to think of anything more exciting than attending your entertaining and fun-filled afternoon, I tried harder and thought of about four hundred things.

I was actually in a Bible-based play once and played the role of "Annoyed about having to do this." My scene involved offering a pot plant (since nobody knew what myrrh was) to a plastic baby Jesus, then standing between "I forgot my costume, so am wearing the teacher's poncho" and "I don't feel very well." Highlights of the play included a nervous donkey with diarrhea, causing "I don't feel very well" to vomit onto the back of Mary's head; and the lighting system, designed to provide a halo effect around the manger, overheating and setting it alight. The teacher, later criticized for dousing an electrical fire with a bucket of water and endangering the lives of children, left the building in tears and the audience in silence. We saw her again only briefly when she came to the school to collect her poncho.

Also, your inference that I am without religion is incorrect, and I am actually torn between two faiths; while your god's promise of eternal life is very persuasive, the Papua New Guinean mud god, Pikkiwoki, is promising a pig and as many coconuts as you can carry.

Regards, David

From: Darryl Robinson
Date: Thursday 11 March 2010 2:52 p.m.
To: David Thorne
Subject: Re: Re: Re: Permission Slip

Hello David

It would be a pity for Seb to miss out on the important message of hope that the story of the resurrection gives, but if you don't want him to attend the presentation on Monday then just tick the other box.

Darryl Robinson, School Chaplain

From: David Thorne
Date: Thursday 11 March 2010 5:09 p.m.
To: Darryl Robinson
Subject: Re: Re: Re: Re: Permission Slip

Dear Darryl,

I understand the importance the resurrection story holds in your particular religion. If I, too, knew some guy that had been killed and placed inside a cave with a rock in front of it, and I visited the cave to find the rock moved and his body gone, the only logical assumption would be that he had risen from the dead and is the Son of God. Once, my friend Simon was rushed to the hospital to have his appendix removed, and I visited him the next day to find his bed empty. I immediately sacrificed a goat and burned a witch in his name, but it turned out that he had not had appendicitis, just needed a good poo and was at home playing PlayStation.

I realize PlayStation was not around in those days, but they probably had the equivalent. A muddy stick or something. I would have said, "Can someone please check if Jesus is at home playing with his muddy stick? If not, then and only then should we all assume, logically, that he has risen from the dead and is the Son of God."

If we accept, though, that Jesus was the son of an Infinite Being capable of anything, he probably did have a PlayStation. Probably a PlayStation 7. I know I have to get my offspring all the latest gadgets. God would have probably said to him, "I was going to wait another two thousand years to give you this, but seeing as you have been good . . . just don't tell your mother about *Grand Theft Auto*."

Also, is it true that Jesus can be stabbed during a sword fight and be OK because of the fact that he can die only if he gets his head chopped off?

Regards, David

From: Darryl Robinson
Date: Friday 12 March 2010 10:13 a.m.
To: David Thorne
Subject: Re: Re: Re: Re: Re: Permission Slip

Nowhere in the Bible does Jesus have a sword fight. Learning the teachings of the Bible is not just about religion. It teaches a set of ethics that are sadly not taught by parents nowadays.

Darryl Robinson, School Chaplain

From: David Thorne
Date: Friday 12 March 2010 2:23 p.m.
To: Darryl Robinson
Subject: Re: Re: Re: Re: Re: Permission Slip

Dear Darryl,

You raise a valid point, and I appreciate your pointing out my
failings as a parent. Practicing a system of ethics based on the
promise of a reward, in your case an afterlife, is certainly preferable
to practicing a system of ethics based on it simply being the right
thing to do.

Many years ago, I lived next door to a Christian named Mr. Stevens.
You could tell he was a Christian, because he had a fish sticker on
his Datsun. He used to wave at us kids from his bathroom window on
hot summer days as we played in the sprinkler. I learned a lot from
Mr. Stevens. Mainly about wrestling holds. The trick is to oil up really
well. I would often lie on his living room rug looking up at the pictures of
sunsets behind quotes from Psalms while waiting for him to unwrap his
legs from around my torso.

Your job would be made much easier if, after making the school
children sit through an hour of church youth group teens dancing, singing
and re-enacting Jewish magic tricks, you simply told them that it was just
a small taste of what hell is like and if they didn't believe in Jesus they
would have to sit through it again. When I was at school, we were forced
to attend a similar presentation. Herded into the gym under the pretense
of free chips, we were assaulted with an hour of hippies playing guitars
and a dance routine featuring some kind of colorful coat and a lot of
looking upward. Because of the air-conditioning in the packed gym not
working and it being a hot day, the hippie wearing the colorful coat
blacked out mid performance and struck his head against the front edge
of the stage, spraying the first row of cross-legged children with blood.
Unconscious, he also urinated. There was a bit of screaming and an

ambulance involved, and everyone agreed it was the best play they had ever seen.

Regards, David

From: Darryl Robinson
Date: Friday 12 March 2010 2:47 p.m.
To: David Thorne
Subject: Re: Re: Re: Re: Re: Re: Re: Permission Slip

Hello David

I don't see what any of that has to do with this play. It's important for children to have balance in their life and spirituality is as important in a childs life as everything else. There's an old saying that life without religion is life without beauty.

Darryl Robinson, School Chaplain

From: David Thorne
Date: Friday 12 March 2010 3:36 p.m.
To: Darryl Robinson
Subject: Re: Re: Re: Re: Re: Re: Re: Re: Permission Slip

Dear Darryl,

I agree completely that balance is an important component of a child's education. I will assume then that you will also be organizing a class excursion to a play depicting the fifteen billion year expansion of the universe from its initial particle soup moments following the big bang through to molecule coalescence, galaxy and planetary formation, and eventually life?

Perhaps your church youth group could put together an interpretive dance routine representing the behavior of Saturn's moon Hyperion, shattered by an ancient collision and falling randomly back together; tugged to and fro by the gravitational pull of Titan, sixteen sister moons, the multibillion-fold moonlets of Saturn's rings, Saturn's gravitational field, companion planets, the variability of Sol, stars, galaxies, neighboring galaxies . . . or possibly not. According to an old saying, there is no beauty in this.

Also, while I understand that the play is to be held outside school grounds because of the fact that it is illegal to present medieval metaphysical propaganda in public schools, it is also my understanding that you are now required by law, as of last year, to go by the title Christian Volunteer rather than School Chaplain. A memo you may have missed or filed in your overflowing "Facts that cease to exist when they are ignored" tray.

Regards, David

From: Darryl Robinson
Date: Monday 15 March 2010 9:22 a.m.
To: David Thorne
Subject: Re: Re: Re: Re: Re: Re: Re: Re: Re: Permission Slip

I'm not going to waste any more time replying to your stupid e-mails. If you don't want your child to attend the play just indicate that on the permission slip.

From: David Thorne
Date: Monday 15 March 2010 11:04 a.m.
To: Darryl Robinson
Subject: Re: Re: Re: Re: Re: Re: Re: Re: Re: Re: Permission Slip

PERMISSION SLIP

Dear Parent/Guardian of _____Seb Thorne_____

On Monday the 22nd of March, classes from year 5 and 6 will be attending a presentation held outside of school grounds at the Mary Richardson Memorial Hall. During the presentation, the true meaning of Easter will be explained in an entertaining and fun filled play performed by members of the Grange Uniting Church youth drama group. Students must have a signed permission slip prior to departure. If you give your child permission to attend this presentation, please sign and return to the school with your child. If you have any questions about the presentation, please call me on ~~(08)~~ or send me an email to darryl~~@~~u

Darryl Robinson ~~School Chaplain~~ *Christian Volunteer*

☑ I give my child permission
☐ I do not give my child permission

to attend the Mary Richardson Memorial Hall on 22.3.2010 for a class presentation.

_____
Parent / Guardian Signature

From: Darryl Robinson
Date: Monday 15 March 2010 2:11 p.m.
To: David Thorne
Subject: No Subject

I will pray for you.

From: David Thorne
Date: Monday 15 March 2010 2:19 p.m.
To: Darryl Robinson
Subject: Re: No Subject

Thanks. Mention that I want a Toyota Prado if you get the chance. A white one. With dark grey leather interior and sat. nav.

Regards, David

From: Darryl Robinson
Date: Tuesday 16 March 2010 9:20 a.m.
To: David Thorne
Subject: Re: Re: No Subject

I've had enough of your nonsense. Dont e-mail me again.

From: GOD
Date: Tuesday 16 March 2010 10:18 a.m.
To: Darryl Robinson
Subject: Word of God

DARRYL, THIS IS GOD. BUY DAVID A TOYOTA PRADO. A WHITE ONE. WITH DARK GREY LEATHER INTERIOR AND SAT. NAV.

From: Darryl Robinson
Date: Tuesday 16 March 2010 2:35 p.m.
To: GOD **Cc:** David Thorne
Subject: Re: Word of God

I'm serious.

From: GOD
Date: Tuesday 16 March 2010 2:48 p.m.
To: Darryl Robinson
Subject: Re: Re: Word of God

OK.

Simon's
good ideas for websites

....

Hello, my name is Simon. I have good ideas for websites all the time. Every single one of my ideas would make lots of money. Do not copy these ideas, because they are mine.

....

everything.com
This would be a website where instead of having to look all over the Internet for what you want, it would all be in the one place. This would effectively end the need for search engines, so I would have to be careful that Google representatives do not kill me in my sleep.

whereaboutsami.com
This would be a website where users can write the name of the city and street they are on, and I would tell them where they are.

onlinepetfrog.com
Instead of buying their own pet frog, users would pay a fee, and I would buy them a frog and look after it. Users could log on anytime to a live webcam, see how their frog is doing, and send live requests for me to wave the frog's hand at the camera or bang on the glass if it is sleeping.

whatkindofcoughisthat.com
A website that contains sound files of different coughs. Each cough would have a description to allow the user to sound match and determine the kind

of cough they have before going to the chemist and buying either dry or wet cough medicine.

yourloungeroom.com

Users would be able take a photo of their lounge room and upload it to the site. Then I would tell them what furniture does not look good.

howdoigettowhereiam.com

This site would contain a link to the page the user is currently on.

whichonetowear.com

Users of this website would take photos of themselves wearing every combination of every article of clothing they own, then upload the images to a user database. Every day, instead of trying on clothing, the user can choose an outfit by simply viewing their choices online.

armbook.com

Similar to Facebook, but people upload photos of their arms.

deceasedlovedones.com

This would be a website where you pay a fee to join and are given your own web page with an empty blog. In the event of their death, users can write a message to their loved ones. Similar setup to prepaid funerals. Loved ones either can log on and check whether the user has left a message for them or can opt to receive an e-mail notifying them when a message has been left.

everyoneschair.com

A website where users can upload a picture of their chair and then if anyone tries to use it they can say, "That's my chair." And if anyone says, "Has it got your name on it?" users can send them a link to their photo of the chair, which will have the caption "This is (user's name)'s chair."

screensavingpage.com

A website that is a black page so that people can go there instead of buying a screensaver.

uploadyourscreen.com

A website where users take a screenshot of their computer screen and upload it so that when they are looking at porn and the boss walks past they can type in the link and go to it instead.

picturesofpegs.com

This website would contain pictures of pegs, allowing the users to have access to pictures of pegs whenever they need them.

amihavingaheartattack.com

A website for people having a heart attack.

Blockbuster Video Pty Ltd
555 Portrush Rd Glenunga SA 5064
Tel (08) 8338 0053
Fax (08) 8338 0048
www.blockbuster.com.au
ABN 992 002 682

4.11.2009

Dear Mr Thorne,

I am writing to advise that movies borrowed on the 14th of October are now three weeks overdue and have accumulated fees of $82. Please return the following movies before they gain further fees.

002190382 Journey to the Centre of the Earth
003103119 Logans Run
008629103 Harold and Kumar Escape from Guantanamo Bay
000721082 Waterworld

Kind regards,
Megan

Megan Roberts
Store Manager

Blockbuster Video Pty Ltd
555 Portrush Rd Glenunga SA 5064
Tel (08) 8338 0053
megan.roberts@blockbuster.com.au
www.blockbuster.com.au

Dear Blockbuster member,
we want our DVDs back

I find it annoying to pay late fees on movies, and I am too lazy to return them on time, which leaves me simply complaining about it. I used to know a guy named Matthew who would sell me copies of the latest movies for five dollars each, but they were all recorded by someone in a cinema with what appeared to be a low-resolution webcam, and epilepsy. Several times during each movie the person would shift positions, or have people walk past in front, and one time filmed the chair in front of him for at least twenty minutes. Matthew's statement was that he did not know the quality before he got them, but in one, the person filming answered his phone with "Hello, Matthew speaking," and when I mentioned it to him, he stopped selling me movies.

From: David Thorne
Date: Sunday 8 November 2009 2:16 p.m.
To: Megan Roberts
Subject: DVDs

Dear Megan,

Thank you for your letter regarding overdue fees. As all four movies were outstanding examples of modern cinematic masterpieces, your assumption that I would wish to retain them in my possession is understandable but incorrect. Please check your records, because these movies were returned, on time, more than three weeks ago. I remember specifically driving there and having my offspring run them in due to the fact that I was wearing shorts and did not want the girl behind the counter to see my white, hairy legs.

Regards, David

From: Megan Roberts
Date: Monday 9 November 2009 11:09 a.m.
To: David Thorne
Subject: Re: DVDs

Hi David. Our computer system indicates otherwise. Please recheck and get back to me.

Kind regards, Megan

From: David Thorne
Date: Monday 9 November 2009 11:36 a.m.
To: Megan Roberts
Subject: Re: Re: DVDs

Dear Megan,

Yes, they are definitely white and hairy. Viewed from the knees down, the similarity to two large albino caterpillars in parallel formation is frightening. People who knew what the word means might describe them as "piliferous," although there is something quite sexy about that word, so perhaps they wouldn't.

Regards, David

From: Megan Roberts
Date: Monday 9 November 2009 1:44 p.m.
To: David Thorne
Subject: Re: Re: Re: DVDs

Hi David

No I mean our records indicate that the DVDs have not been returned. Please check and return as soon as possible.

Kind regards, Megan

From: David Thorne
Date: Monday 9 November 2009 4:19 p.m.
To: Megan Roberts
Subject: Re: Re: Re: Re: DVDs

Dear Megan,

With the possible exception of *Harold and Kumar Escape from Guantanamo Bay,* the movies were not worth watching, let alone stealing. In *Logan's Run,* for example, the computer crashed at the end when presented with conflicting facts, and blew up, destroying the entire city. When my computer crashes I carry on a little bit and have a cigarette while it is rebooting. I don't have to search through rubble for my loved ones. The same programmers probably designed the Blockbuster "returned or not" database.

Also, while one would assume the title *Journey to the Center of the Earth* to be a metaphor, the movie was actually set in the center of the earth, which, being a solid core of iron with temperatures exceeding 4,300°C and pressures of 3,900 tons per square centimeter, does not seem very likely. *Waterworld* was actually pretty good, though.

My favorite bit was when they were on the water, but the scene when Kevin Costner negotiated for peace, ending the war between fish and mankind moments before the whale army attacked, was also very good.

Regards, David

From: Megan Roberts
Date: Tuesday 10 November 2009 3:57 p.m.
To: David Thorne
Subject: Re: Re: Re: Re: Re: DVDs

David

The DVDs are listed as not returned. If you cant locate the DVDs, you will be charged for the replacement cost.

Megan

From: David Thorne
Date: Tuesday 10 November 2009 5:12 p.m.
To: Megan Roberts
Subject: Re: Re: Re: Re: Re: Re: DVDs

Dear Megan,

I have checked pricing at the DVD Warehouse, and the cost of replacing your lost movies with new ones is as follows:

Harold and Kumar Escape from Guantanamo Bay $7.95
Waterworld $4.95
Journey to the Center of the Earth $9.95
Logan's Run $12.95

I have no idea why *Logan's Run* is the most expensive of the four movies, as it was definitely the worst. Have you seen it? I wouldn't pay $12.95 for that. I would use the money to buy a good movie instead. Probably something with Steven Seagal in it. The entire premise comprised of living a utopian and carefree lifestyle with only three drawbacks—wearing seventies jumpsuits, living in what looks like a giant shopping center, and not being allowed to live past thirty.

This would seem logical, though, as I would not want a bunch of old people hanging around complaining about their arthritis while I am trying to relax at the shopping center in my jumpsuit and trying not to think about the computer crashing.

I was recently forced to do volunteer work at an aged care hospital. Footage of these people during Tuesday-night line dancing could be used as an advertisement for the *Logan's Run* solution. The only good aspect of working there was that I halved their medication, pocketing and selling the remainder, explaining the computer listed that as their dose and they were welcome to check, knowing their abject fear of anything produced after the eighteenth century would prevent them from doing so. I also swapped my Sanyo fourteen-inch portable television for their Panasonic wide-screen plasma while they were sleeping, explaining that it had always been that way and their senility was simply playing up due to the reduced dosage of drugs.

Regards, David

From: Megan Roberts
Date: Wednesday 11 November 2009 1:21 p.m.
To: David Thorne
Subject: Re: Re: Re: Re: Re: Re: Re: DVDs

Hi David

I have not seen those movies so I don't know what you are talking about. I prefer romantic comedies. If you have the movies we can't rent them so we lose money and the fees are based on what we we would have made from renting them and we also have to purchase movies through our suppliers not from DVD Warehouse.

Megan

From: David Thorne
Date: Wednesday 11 November 2009 3:28 p.m.
To: Megan Roberts
Subject: Re: Re: Re: Re: Re: Re: Re: Re: DVDs

Dear Megan,

I myself am also a huge fan of romantic comedies. Perhaps we could watch one together. I have a new Panasonic wide-screen plasma. My favorite romantic comedy is *Fatal Instinct,* although it did not contain enough robots or explosions, in my opinion, and I was therefore unable to truly identify with the main characters on a personal and emotional level. Recently, I was tricked into watching *The Notebook,* which was about geese. Lots of geese. It also had something to do with an old lady who conveniently lost her memory, so she could not remember being a whore throughout the entire film. I don't recall a lot of it, because I was too busy being cross about watching it. In a utopian future society she would have been hunted down and killed at thirty.

In regard to the late fees, I understand the amount is based on what you lose by not being able to rent the movies out. You probably had people lined up around the block waiting to rent *Logan's Run.* For eighty-two dollars, though, I could have purchased six copies of it from DVD Warehouse or, as I have heard he is a bit strapped for cash, had Kevin Costner visit my house in person and re-enact key scenes from *Waterworld* in the bathroom.

Regards, David

From: Megan Roberts
Date: Thursday 12 November 2009 3:16 p.m.
To: David Thorne
Subject: Re: Re: Re: Re: Re: Re: Re: Re: Re: DVDs

Hi David.

Restocking fees are:

    002190382 Journey to the Center of the Earth $9.30
    003103119 Logans Run $7.90
    008629103 Harold and Kumar Escape from Guantanamo Bay $6.30
    000721082 Waterworld $5.70

Total: $29.20—I have deleted your late fees and noted on the computer that the amount owed is for the replacement movies not fees.

Kind regards, Megan

From: David Thorne
Date: Thursday 12 November 2009 7:42 p.m.
To: Megan Roberts
Subject: Re: Re: Re: Re: Re: Re: Re: Re: Re: Re: DVDs

Dear Megan,

Those prices seem reasonable. I do not want *Logan's Run* but will pick up the other three when I come in next.

Regards, David

From: Megan Roberts
Date: Friday 13 November 2009 12:51 p.m.
To: David Thorne
Subject: Re: Re: Re: Re: Re: Re: Re: Re: Re: Re: Re: DVDs

What? The $29.20 is the cost of the replacement DVDs for the store.

Megan

From: David Thorne
Date: Friday 13 November 2009 1:15 p.m.
To: Megan Roberts
Subject: Re: Re: Re: Re: Re: Re: Re: Re: Re: Re: Re: Re: DVDs

Dear Megan,

That makes more sense. I was wondering what I was going to do with two copies of each movie.

Regards, David

From: Megan Roberts
Date: Friday 13 November 2009 2:33 p.m.
To: David Thorne
Subject: Re: Re: Re: Re: Re: Re: Re: Re: Re: Re: Re: Re: Re: DVDs

What do you mean by 2 copies? Are you saying you found the movies?

Megan

From: David Thorne
Date: Friday 13 November 2009 2:57 p.m.
To: Megan Roberts
Subject: Re: Re: Re: Re: Re: Re: Re: Re: Re: Re: Re: Re: Re: Re: DVDs

Dear Megan,

Yes, they were on top of my fridge the whole time. Unfortunately I have a blind spot that prevents me from seeing this area of the kitchen, as it is also where I keep my pile of unpaid bills. Last night I slept on the kitchen floor with the fridge door open because my air conditioner was broken and the temperature outside exceeded that of the center of the earth. As my fridge emits a high pitched "beep" every thirty seconds when left open, the vibrations from this caused the DVDs to wriggle forward over the span of many hours before toppling from the edge, and I awoke to find them beside me on the pillow. As you have already waived the late fees, I will drop them off tonight and we will call it even.

Regards, David

From: Megan Roberts
Date: Friday 13 November 2009 3:43 p.m.
To: David Thorne
Subject: Re: Re: Re: Re: Re: Re: Re: Re: Re: Re: Re: Re: Re: Re: DVDs

Ok.

Hello, my name is Shannon,
and I eat like a snake

Due to an extendable jaw and highly acidic saliva levels, I have found that consuming an orange whole and digesting it over the span of many hours, like a snake, requires almost no effort at all.

I once ate a rock melon, but of course that took many days to digest. People sometimes assume when they see a hint of orange in my mouth that I am wearing a fashionable form of braces or afflicted with a medical condition requiring me to wear a mouthguard at all times, possibly in case of falling over during a seizure or maybe even that sleeping illness you see in movies sometimes. Of course I cannot actually move or do anything while I am digesting, but this has not affected my work, as I can still move my eyes, allowing me to look out the window and keep an eye on the petty cash tin.

Shannon having lunch

A snake digesting a pig

Shannon's blanket of security.

Due to there being no petty cash left, with which Shannon was planning to buy her lunch, Shannon initiates Operation Lunch Money with the unveiling of her new Blanket of Security System (BOSS). The petty cash protection vehicle features Internet access for downloading iTunes and windows for looking out of.

Working out with Jeff
at two hundred and ten dollars per visit

I keep telling myself that I should get fit, but then I see people that I know and work with starting exercise routines and becoming boring, talking about "reps" and reading out the amount of calories from food wrappers as if anybody cares. A year after going to the gym and becoming experts on the amount of water they should drink in a day, they are just as flabby as when they started but less interesting. As I am constantly told I am too skinny, last year I paid four hundred and twenty dollars to join a gym. I attended twice: the first time for almost an hour; the second, only fifteen minutes, when it dawned on me that 1) the level of fitness of the people attending the gym was inversely proportional to the level of intelligence and 2) my instructor was not wearing anything under his Spandex bike pants and the wet semen spot would, in all probability, brush against me if I stayed there any longer.

From: Jeff Peters
Date: Wednesday 8 April 2009 10:22 a.m.
To: David Thorne
Subject: Membership Renewal Due

Dear David

This is a friendly reminder to let you know your gym membership expired last week. Your membership is important to us and we would like to take this opportunity to show our appreciation by offering you a 20% discount on your membership renewal. We look forward to seeing you again soon.

All the best, Jeff Peters

From: David Thorne
Date: Wednesday 8 April 2009 1:37 p.m.
To: Jeff Peters
Subject: Re: Membership Renewal Due

Dear Jeff,

Thank you for your friendly reminder and the kind offer to reduce my membership by 20 percent. I own a calculator but I could not work out how to do percentages on it, so have estimated that I save around $372.10 off the normal price of $420.00. Please confirm that this is correct, and I will renew my membership immediately. Also, do I get a Fitness First sports bag with a towel and drinking bottle included in the price? I own my own leg warmers and headband.

Regards, David

From: Jeff Peters
Date: Thursday 9 April 2009 10:01 a.m.
To: David Thorne
Subject: Re: Re: Membership Renewal Due

Hello David

How did you come to that amount? Our half year membership fees are actually $460 but with the 20% discount as an existing member your renewing membership fee would be only $368 for the six months saving you almost $100 off the normal price. We are not Fitness First so do not have those bags.

Cheers, Jeff

From: David Thorne
Date: Thursday 9 April 2009 10:18 a.m.
To: Jeff Peters
Subject: Re: Re: Re: Membership Renewal Due

Dear Jeff,

Do I get free shipping with that?

Regards, David

From: Jeff Peters
Date: Thursday 9 April 2009 12:48 p.m.
To: David Thorne
Subject: Re: Re: Re: Re: Membership Renewal Due

Free shipping with what? The $368 covers your membership fees for six months.

From: David Thorne
Date: Thursday 9 April 2009 2:26 p.m.
To: Jeff Peters
Subject: Re: Re: Re: Re: Re: Membership Renewal Due

Dear Jeff,

By the power of Grayskull, that is a lot of money, but I admit to being in desperate need of increasing my body strength. My ten-year-old child often turns the taps off in the bathroom very tightly, so I have to go several days without washing. I feel bad constantly having to ask the lady from next door to come over and loosen them for me, what with her arthritis and limited wheelchair access to my apartment.

To be honest, I originally joined your gym with full intentions of attending every few days, but after waiting in vain for someone to offer me steroids, I began to suspect that was not going to happen; and the realization that I may have to exercise instead was, quite frankly, horrifying. My aversion to work, along with the fact one of your employees, Justin, was rather rude, telling me to "lift this," "push that," dulled my initial enthusiasm of becoming muscular, and I stopped attending.

Regards, David

From: Jeff Peters
Date: Friday 10 April 2009 9:17 a.m.
To: David Thorne
Subject: Re: Re: Re: Re: Re: Re: Membership Renewal Due

Hello David

Not sure how to take your e-mail, nobody here would offer you steroids, it is illegal and none of our staff would do this. Justin is one of our most experienced trainers, and if you found him rude while he was trying to be helpful and just doing his job, then there are plenty of other gyms you could look at joining instead.

Cheers, Jeff

From: David Thorne
Date: Friday 10 April 2009 10:02 a.m.
To: Jeff Peters
Subject: Re: Re: Re: Re: Re: Re: Re: Membership Renewal Due

Dear Jeff,

Yes, I have noticed that there are many gyms in my area. I assume the low qualification requirements of fitness trainers means that there is an oversupply of these buffed but essentially otherwise purposeless professionals. I knew a guy in high school who couldn't talk very well and collected sticks; he used to call the teacher "mum," and during recess we would give him money to dance. Then sell him sticks to get our money back. He went on to become a fitness instructor, so I view gyms as kind of like those factories that provide a community service by employing people with Down's syndrome to lick stamps and pack boxes. Except with more Spandex, obviously.

Regards, David

From: Jeff Peters
Date: Friday 10 April 2009 10:32 a.m.
To: David Thorne
Subject: Re: Re: Re: Re: Re: Re: Re: Re: Membership Renewal Due

Go fuck yourself.

From: David Thorne
Date: Friday 10 April 2009 11:38 a.m.
To: Jeff Peters
Subject: Re: Re: Re: Re: Re: Re: Re: Re: Re: Membership Renewal Due

Dear Jeff,

I was, at first, quite surprised at your response. One minute you are inviting me to renew my membership and asking me for money, and the next, insulting me. After doing a little research, however, I have learned that mood swings are an expected side effect of steroid abuse. As another side effect is a reduction in the size of your penis, this gives you understandable cause to be an angry person. I have also learned that Spandex contains carcinogenic properties, so this does not bode well for you and your shiny friends. If I woke up one morning and my penis was a quarter of the size AND I had testicular cancer, I would probably take my anger out on those around me as well. There are probably support groups or websites that could help you manage your problem more effectively and picture-based books available on the subject. When I am angry I like to listen to music by Linkin Park.

The added angst and desire to cut myself works similarly to the way firefighters fight forest fires by burning off sections, effectively canceling each other out and finding myself at peace. I understand that you guys usually listen to Pet Shop Boys or Frankie Goes to Hollywood, but this may be worth a try.

Regards, David

From: Jeff Peters
Date: Friday 10 April 2009 1:04 p.m.
To: David Thorne
Subject: Re: Re: Re: Re: Re: Re: Re: Re: Re: Re: Membership
Renewal Due

DO NOT E-MAIL ME AGAIN

From: David Thorne
Date: Friday 10 April 2009 1:15 p.m.
To: Jeff Peters
Subject: Re: Re: Re: Re: Re: Re: Re: Re: Re: Re: Re: Membership
Renewal Due

OK.

From: Jeff Peters
Date: Friday 10 April 2009 1:25 p.m.
To: David Thorne
Subject: Re: Re: Re: Re: Re: Re: Re: Re: Re: Re: Re: Membership
Renewal Due

Is that you being a smartarse or agreeing not to e-mail me again?

From: David Thorne
Date: Friday 10 April 2009 1:32 p.m.
To: Jeff Peters
Subject: Re: Re: Re: Re: Re: Re: Re: Re: Re: Re: Re: Re:
Membership Renewal Due

The middle one.

Interview with Flight Commander Thorne

Flight Commander Thorne has been part of three successful space missions, including the recent delivery of new flannels to the International Space Station.

Thank you for joining us today and congratulations on your recent successful mission aboard Discovery. *Could you explain to us what it was like to be in space?*

Yes, I can. It was a lot smaller than I expected. I used to try to take in the fact that earth is spinning around a tiny sun, which is just one of billions in a tiny cluster that makes up just a bit of our Milky Way, which is one of billions of galaxies with billions of billions of kilometers between them, and I would get massive headaches and overwhelming feelings of insignificance with bouts of depression that ultimately led to the breakdown of my third marriage, but when you get up there you realize that there is not that much to it.

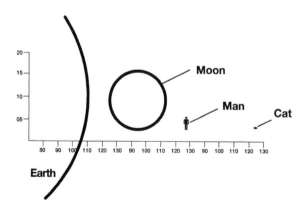

How long does it take to reach your mission destination?

Good question. Contrary to popular belief, distances in space are pretty close—rockets are seriously fast, so it takes only about 12 minutes to get to the moon and an hour or so to Mars, etc. It was assumed the distances were greater because of our mistaken calculations in regard to the size of objects in space. The moon for example was thought to be 384,633 kilometers away due to the calculation of it having a radius of 3,476 kilometers, but in fact, it is only 16 kilometers up with a radius of 2.3 kilometers. I myself walked the complete circumference of the moon in under an hour, and that included stopping often to look at interesting rocks. If I throw one of the rocks out into space it will travel through the void for eternity. I usually do this three or four hundred times each visit. Sometimes I spit on the rocks first, knowing my DNA may travel to another world countless light years away and fertilize a new beginning for mankind.

Could you explain the functions of your suit?

Yes, the suits are pretty cool, aren't they? They may look uncomfortable but are actually like wearing a large fluffy quilt and can be put on or taken off in under thirty seconds. I quite often wear mine around the house when I am ironing, mowing the lawn, or popping down to the shops to get some milk. The controls on the front may seem complicated but simply control the bass, treble, and volume of the built-in MP3 player.

How do you prepare for each mission takeoff?

We try to get a good night's sleep beforehand, making sure everything is packed and we haven't forgotten anything. Once the ignition spark hits twenty tons of solid rocket fuel, we can't turn around and go to the shop. On one mission, no one remembered to bring cigarettes, so the whole trip everyone was bitching and grumpy—I had a packet in my suit, but I had to hide them and only smoke in the toilet or everyone would have wanted

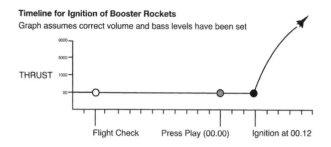

Timeline for Ignition of Booster Rockets
Graph assumes correct volume and bass levels have been set

THRUST

9000
5000
1000
00

Flight Check   Press Play (00.00)   Ignition at 00.12

them. Music is also very important, we strap in, run a prelaunch flight check, then press the ignition switch, which hits us with 9,000 G of thrust at exactly twelve seconds into the Linkin Park track "With You," which is fed at full volume through our helmet speakers.

As commander, you must rely on a dedicated and highly skilled crew to ensure each successful mission.

You would assume that wouldn't you? You would think that a team would support their commander and encourage his leadership and support his decisions, wouldn't you? You would expect there to be no bickering about little things or saying stuff behind people's backs, wouldn't you? Good teamwork comes from listening to your commander; that's why there are ranks. Some people just do not understand that there is no "i" in team. I tell them that the word "team" stands for "terrifically exciting aims met" and had T-shirts made, but they didn't wear them.

Thank you, Commander, for taking the time out of your busy schedule to come and talk to us today. Is there any last message you would like to give to our students?

No problem, I wasn't doing much today. Well, if there were one message I would like to give to the kids of today, it would be not to do drugs. They may seem fun at the time and yes they may enhance sex and make music sound better, but they can be expensive unless you know the right people, so you would be better off buying books and pens and stuff. Space may be big, but it's nowhere near as big as your potential if you have pens and other writing implements that you may need.

NASA Space Facts

The sun is twenty times brighter than a sixty-watt light bulb and generates twice the heat of a potter's kiln.

Russian astronaut Mikael Novas has been living on the ISS for eight years and collects erotica.

You can make your own rocket fuel at home using a three-to-one ratio of chlorine and brake fluid.

Space shuttle *Endeavor* contains living quarters for eighteen people and features a gymnasium and squash courts.

Due to the shuttle taking off in the Florida swamps, several hundred ducks are incinerated during each launch. NASA employees often eat them following a successful takeoff.

It is obviously
that your a foggot

Sometimes people e-mail me to tell me how their day is going; other times they e-mail me to tell me that I am a dickhead and my website is stupid, which I am already aware of due to many preceding e-mails stating the same thing. I don't harbor behind a fake name, and my e-mail address is clearly listed, so it is a simple process for people like George to express their opinions to me; but as I never initiate an e-mail correspondence, simply reply, I am not always sure why they bother.

If I were heteroflexible, I am pretty sure I would already be aware of the fact; and if I'm not, stating that I am is in error, so either way it is a pointless exercise. I don't e-mail random people telling them that they have a pet cat named Charles on the off chance they do and are not aware of it.

From: George Lewis
Date: Thursday 2 September 2010 6:51 p.m.
To: David Thorne
Subject: No Subject

I have read your website and it is obviously that your a foggot.

From: David Thorne
Date: Thursday 2 September 2010 8:07 p.m.
To: George Lewis
Subject: Re: No Subject

Dear George,

Thank you for your e-mail. While I have no idea what a "foggot" is, I will assume it is a term of endearment and appreciate your taking time out from calculating launch trajectories or removing temporal lobe tumors to contact me with such. I have attached a signed photo as per your request.

Regards, David

From: George Lewis
Date: Thursday 2 September 2010 8:49 p.m.
To: David Thorne
Subject: Re: Re: No Subject

I didnt ask for a photo fag. and I meant faggot you homo so you can shove your signed photo up your ass. You would probably enjoy that. LOL!!!! Go suck your boyfriends dick in a gay club.

From: David Thorne
Date: Thursday 2 September 2010 9:17 p.m.
To: George Lewis
Subject: Re: Re: Re: No Subject

Dear George,

While I do not have a boyfriend, I do have a friend who is homosexual, and I once asked him, "Do you ever think about having sex with me because you are gay?" to which he replied, "Do you ever think about having sex with Rosie O'Donnell because you are straight? Same thing." If I were inclined to have a boyfriend, I would select one my height and weight to save having to readjust the driver's seat position. I am not interested in doubling my wardrobe, as I wear the same outfit every day to facilitate speedy identification should I ever be in a boating accident.

Although I have never been to a gay club as such, when I was about ten, a friend and I constructed a clubhouse in my backyard using timber stolen from a building site down the street. Our club, which we named The Kiss Club due to a certain band being popular at the time, employed an intensive entry exam in which the applicant had to know all the words to "Love Gun" and not be a girl. As we had no other friends and knew no girls apart from my sister, this made sense at the time. The next day after school, having managed to recruit several new members by promising laminated membership cards and changing the entry exam to "Knowing the names of the band members," we all rode to my place to participate in our first club meeting only to discover my sister, outraged by the "No girls" rule and armed with four liters of paint left over from a recent bedroom redesign, had painted the clubhouse pink and added "ing" to the end of the word "Kiss."

Also, despite your inference, I have managed, up to this point, to avoid putting most things in my bottom. Primarily due to the possibility that I might enjoy it, get carried away, and move on to watermelons or midsize family autos. When I was about eight, I drew a face on my hand and practiced kissing it, which I will admit is a little gay; and I have often thought there would be advantages to homosexuality, such as Abercrombie & Fitch reward points, successful couch fabric selection capabilities, and the gift of dance. With or without a top on. This would be extremely useful if I needed five hundred dollars and saw a poster advertising a dance competition with a first prize of five hundred dollars.

Regards, David

From: George Lewis
Date: Thursday 2 September 2010 9:33 p.m.
To: David Thorne
Subject: Re: Re: Re: Re: No Subject

If you livd close by gaycunt I would be over your place with 5 friends tonight.

From: David Thorne
Date: Thursday 2 September 2010 10:08 p.m.
To: George Lewis
Subject: Re: Re: Re: Re: Re: No Subject

Dear George,

I knew we would get along well. We have known each other for only one day and already you are organizing a party. I am not sure where Gaycunt is, but if I did "livd close by" to it, I would definitely be up for that.

We could all sit outside on banana lounges discussing the best way to rebuild a 4WD transmission and agree, through shared stories of conquests supporting our assertions, that there is no basis to the proposition that those least assured of their persuasions are the first to condemn others for theirs. Although the ideal would be for everyone to be capable of love without fear, restraint, or obligation, clearly this does not apply to homosexuals.

At no time during the night would you comment on how much you liked my Abercrombie & Fitch pants or ask, "Is that a Marcel Breuer couch? I love the fabric selection," and when we danced, we would all leave our tops on.

Regards, David

From: George Lewis
Date: Friday 3 September 2010 1:18 p.m.
To: David Thorne
Subject: Re: Re: Re: Re: Re: No Subject

no fag I live in Charleston west virginia the best country in the world. I wasnt sying it would be a party. we would smash your fucking skull in and if you are calling me a fag you can get fucked becasue I have a girlfriend.

From: David Thorne
Date: Friday 3 September 2010 1:56 p.m.
To: George Lewis
Subject: Yeehaw, y'all

Dear George,

Is she also your sister? I checked out her photos on your Facebook page, and while she is not exactly my type, I accept that other people have different preferences. Even when those preferences include facial tattoos and stretch pants constructed from sufficient material to shelter a small village. And their livestock.

Some men enjoy dancing with other men without their tops on while others prefer the company of a woman two KFC Family Buckets away from upsetting the planet's rotational axis.

I read somewhere that Eskimos prefer women of girth as they provide warmth at night. I have seen the size of those igloos, though, and there is no way your girlfriend would make it through the opening. You could probably just construct one around her and despite the hassle of having to trudge out into the snow every day to catch and prepare the eighty seals required to maintain her mass, it would be like a kiln in there. If I were an Eskimo, I would build my igloo next to a supermarket or on a tropical beach.

Regards, David

From: George Lewis
Date: Friday 3 September 2010 2:01 p.m.
To: David Thorne
Subject: Re: Yeehaw, y'all

She isnt fat you fag. and that she got that tattoo is a teardrop becasue her family is dead.

From: David Thorne
Date: Friday 3 September 2010 2:06 p.m.
To: George Lewis
Subject: Re: Re: Yeehaw, y'all

Did she eat them?

From: George Lewis
Date: Friday 3 September 2010 2:32 p.m.
To: David Thorne
Subject: Re: Re: Re: Yeehaw, y'all

Get fucked fag her family they died in a traffic accident. have some respect. Go put some more gel in your hair and dye it balck like a emo skinny fag. And how can you see my facebook page pictures?

From: David Thorne
Date: Friday 3 September 2010 3:02 p.m.
To: George Lewis
Subject: Re: Re: Re: Re: Yeehaw, y'all

Dear George,

Yes, I have heard those motorhomes can be a bitch to steer. Especially around tight corners during a police chase or moonshine run. I will concede to 50 percent of your description of me as a "skinny fag" being correct. If our bodies are temples, mine would be a heavily shelled Iranian mosque express. To rectify this, I have instigated a fitness and weight training regimen. Once a week I carry two heavy garbage bags out to the sidewalk and jog back. As this week was my first session and I did not want to overexert myself, I took the car. Obviously with a few breaks in between to rehydrate and stretch.

Although hardly an emo, I understand their pain. If I looked in the mirror and saw an anorexic version of Pugsley Adams staring back at me, I would probably start cutting myself as well. I will admit to having dyed my hair once, though. The product, misrepresented as "Natural Black" instead of "Astro Boy Black," turned my hair as dark as an adequate simile describing just how black it actually was and stained my forehead and ears purple. In an attempt to blend the color, I rubbed the remainder of the mixture onto my face, figuring it might look like a tan. I spent the following two weeks telling people that I could not leave the house due to agoraphobia, an illness usually self-diagnosed by the unemployed as an excuse to stay home and masturbate or play Wii.

I have access to your Facebook page due to the friend request you accepted from the Oscar Wilde profile I constructed yesterday.

I assumed the name would hold no relevance to you and, consistency being the last refuge of the unimaginative, I typed "Redneck wearing baseball cap" into Google images to locate a photo you would identify and feel comfortable with.

Regards, David

From: George Lewis
Date: Friday 3 September 2010 4:48 p.m.
To: David Thorne
Subject: Re: Re: Re: Re: Re: Yeehaw, y'all

Thats fraud. I will report you to the police and to facebook fag. i would shoot you in the face with my .32 if you were here right now.

From: David Thorne
Date: Friday 3 September 2010 5:19 p.m.
To: George Lewis
Subject: tarded

Dear George,

Yes, I'm fairly certain there is a worldwide criminal investigation network dedicated solely to bringing those who construct fake Facebook profiles to justice. I believe the punishment is tar and feathering in most parts of the world except West Virginia, where you are stripped naked, oiled up, and chased around a paddock while wearing a pig mask.

Apparently, in West Virginia this is also known as a "date." Variations include substituting the paddock with a motorhome or the person with an actual pig. Or in your case, both.

Also, as it is probably far more acceptable for men in West Virginia to hold guns than hands, I will assume the phrase "shooting me in the face with my .32" is not a euphemism.

Regards, David

From: George Lewis
Date: Friday 3 September 2010 7:04 p.m.
To: David Thorne
Subject: Re: tarded

Ive deleted you from my facebook and reported you. i hope you die of aids fag. Dont bothering e-mailing me again becasue I wont read it.

From: David Thorne
Date: Friday 3 September 2010 7:12 p.m.
To: George Lewis
Subject: dneck

Yes you will.

From: George Lewis
Date: Friday 3 September 2010 7:16 p.m.
To: David Thorne
Subject: Re: dneck

No I fucking wont fag

Scientific Model showing Tom's head in relation to planetary mass

Tom in his car

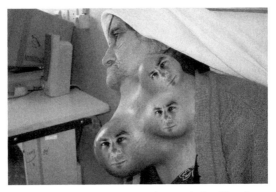

Tom's head badly photoshopped onto a lady with goiters

Breakthrough
medical operation
brings new hope for Thomas

....

It was Champagne all round last night in celebration of the medical break-through that, despite previous diagnostics, may indeed cure Thomas of the rare condition that has caused his head to swell to unimagined proportions.

....

Dr. Hermine Bergmann is thrilled with the results. "We have been able to reduce the swelling by 85 percent, bringing his head down to the size of a small family car or large hatchback, similar to the Renault my husband recently bought me," she said. "We have him wearing a two-person inflat-able boat as a hat to avoid any further damage, but we hope to have his head down to a size where he will be able to drive his convertible with the roof up."

Thomas's family is extremely pleased at the breakthrough: "I thought his head was just going to get bigger and bigger till it exploded," said his father. "He'd come over and sit down in front of the telly, and no one could see a bloody thing past his great hairy weather balloon of a head. It was fucking incredible—you should have seen it. I would have taken photos but didn't have a wide-angle lens."

Medical staff first believed it may have been simply a large tumor with a face, but this was disproven when some movement resembling motor skills was observed. "The operation was touch-and-go there for a while," said Dr. Bergmann. "We simply did not have medical instruments designed to cut through that amount of mass; even the industrial laser brought in especially for the operation struggled to get through the eighteen meters of solid limestone, but the patient is doing well and looking forward to one day being able to wear his trucker hats again."

Physicists have expressed relief about the news, as it was widely considered fact among the scientific field that Thomas's head, if allowed to expand further, would develop its own gravitational field, affecting planetary rotation.

Hello, my name is Scott,
and I have a blog

My blog contains the wittiest stuff on the Internet. I have had over five hits on my blog during the time it has been running, and not all of those have been people I asked to go there.

Because I am a professional blog writer, I recently upgraded my Amstrad CPC 464 to an appropriate system befitting my role. Using my wife's credit card, I purchased fifteen mainframe computer systems but have ordered an additional twenty-five computers, as no matter how full my hard drives become, people keep putting new porn on the Internet. I have no idea how they expect me to keep up. I feel like Captain Picard commanding the *Enterprise* when I work, and sometimes I wear my *Star Trek* uniform when my wife is out. My favorite character from *Star Trek* is Wesley. Once during a freak storm, the electricity in our house went out and I was unable to access my hard drives for more than five hours. My testicles grew to the size of small watermelons, and I was rushed to the hospital. While I was recovering in Ward 7G, I made friends with a small boy named Ross in the bed next to me. He died from cancer the next day, so I took his Sony PSP.

As a professional blog writer of the wittiest stuff on the Internet, I recently decided to quit my job as head assistant chef in charge of pickles at McDonald's and focus full time on my writing career. Due to my unique creative spark and rapier sharp wit, my blog has had unprecedented success, and just this week I had another hit. Being a professional blog writer is not all Moët and chicken nuggets, though. Due to server and hosting fees, I made minus four hundred and ninety dollars last financial year, but my wife works three jobs and has a credit card, so it all balances out.

If I had friends, they would often ask me, "Scott, what is the secret behind your Champagne-quality comedy?" and I would explain to them that it is just a gift and that some people are naturally born with an incredible creative spark while others just get to read it. Recently, I wrote about the time a bee flew in my car window and then flew back out. It was so funny, and when I posted a link to it on *World of Warcraft,* a level 54 dwarf wrote back saying, "Awesome man," which made my day. Once when I was online in my dwarf clan, I met a level 41 dwarf named Cindy, and we fell in love despite her being below my status. I would send her poetry about *Warcraft* and she would edit it for me. As my wife works 180-hour weeks, this gave me plenty of opportunity to organize a liaison with Cindy in real life. After arranging to meet, I packed my dwarf costume and battle-ax and used my wife's credit card to buy a bus ticket to the town Cindy lived in. As it turned out, Cindy was actually a real dwarf. And a man. We still made love so as not to waste the money I had spent, but I left feeling deceived and only partly satisfied. Why can't people just be honest?

Dividing my time between writing professionally on my blog and online as Scott the Invincible is not my only creative outlet. I am also a professional cartoonist. I am much better than Carl Schultz; my ideas are more clever and creative. I would describe my art as cutting edge with my ears to the street, and if you don't get my cartoons then "Yo momma" to you, nigga. Here is one of my best cartoons, when I originally posted it my hits went up 400 percent, and all four people said that it was unlike any professional material they had ever seen before.

The cartoon above is funny on two levels, which makes it lateral. First, I was looking at porn but said that I wasn't, so this is like British comedy and brilliant in itself without the rest. Second, I said, "Make it so," which is what Captain Picard says in *Star Trek*—and I was wearing my Star Trek uniform when I said it. Do you get it? It is probably too clever for you.

If I could give one word of advice to anybody wanting to be a professional blog writer like me, it would be to realize that it does not matter what the subject is; the important thing is how I feel about it. Balance is also important, I find that the best ratio is to have 90 percent of the stories be about me and how I feel about things and the remaining 10 percent linking to stories about me and how I feel about things.

Lucius caught
in Nigerian e-mail sex scam

Local captain of most teams, including the Lucius fan club, is safe after his "safari to riches" became a living nightmare. Replying to the e-mail was his first mistake. A mistake that would cost Lucius more than the amount he gave to Mr. Bandabaloobi.

"Mr. Bandabaloobi told me he was from the Nigerian Bank," said Lucius. "We first met when he wrote me an e-mail explaining he needed me to transfer three million dollars out of the country because a rich old guy had died and the government was going to keep the money unless I could help and for this I would receive a percentage.

"I gave them my account details and bought a plane ticket to Nigeria to meet Mr. Bandabaloobi and sign the transfer papers.

"Once I arrived I was beaten and taken to a small hotel room on the outskirts of town. I was stripped and kissed by dark and very hairy men. One of the men, named Carl, was very gentle and told me he loved me, but the others were rough. So very rough. I struggled and told them I was a friend of Mr. Bandabaloobi, but they tied me up and took turns kissing my

beautiful body, touching me, and making me do things I had sometimes thought about and imagined but had never expected to really happen, because I am straight. The fact that one of the men looked like a black version of my dad kind of freaked me out, and Carl turned out to be huge, but like I said, he was very gentle and we just took things really slow. He's cool; we have swapped e-mails since. Nothing gay, though, cause he knows I am straight.

"Having survived the ordeal and returned home, my only regret is that I missed my meeting with Mr. Bandabaloobi and didn't get to see any African animals like giraffes and lions and those little things that peek up really quick and look around and then pop back down really quick. They are really cool. They are like those little dogs that live on the prairie. I can't remember what those ones are called either, but they look a little bit like otters. They don't live in water like otters, though; they live on the prairies. No, I don't know what a prairie is."

Missing Missy
I was up all night in tears

I am not a big fan of cats. I do not hate them; I just have no interest in them whatsoever. If I visit your house, I do not want to pat your cat, sit on the couch where it has been, or have you make me a sandwich after patting it. I didn't want that sandwich, anyway. The Maxwell House coffee was bad enough, and when you smelled the milk to see if it was still OK, despite being a week past its use-by date, I saw your nose touch the carton. I actually rescued a cat once. I was walking across a bridge, over a river that was flooding, when I heard mewing and saw a frantic cat being pulled along. I picked up a fairly hefty branch and threw it over the rail to where the cat was. I did not see it after that, but I am pretty sure it would have climbed on and ridden the branch to safety.

From: Shannon Walkley
Date: Monday 21 June 2010 9:15 a.m.
To: David Thorne
Subject: Poster

Hi. I opened the screen door yesterday and my cat got out and has been missing since then so I was wondering if you are not to busy you could make a poster for me. It has to be A4 and I will photocopy it and put it around my suburb this afternoon.

This is the only photo of her I have she answers to the name Missy and is black and white and about 8 months old. missing on Harper street and my phone number. Thanks Shan.

From: David Thorne
Date: Monday 21 June 2010 9:26 a.m.
To: Shannon Walkley
Subject: Re: Poster

Dear Shannon,

That is shocking news. Luckily I was sitting down when I read your e-mail and not half way up a ladder or tree. How are you holding up? I am surprised you managed to attend work at all, what with thinking about Missy out there, cold, frightened, and alone . . . possibly lying on the side of the road, her back legs squashed by a vehicle, calling out, "Shannon, where are you?"

Although I have two clients expecting completed work this afternoon, I will, of course, drop everything and do whatever it takes to facilitate the speedy return of Missy.

Regards, David

From: Shannon Walkley
Date: Monday 21 June 2010 9:37 a.m.
To: David Thorne
Subject: Re: Re: Poster

yeah ok thanks. I know you dont like cats but I am really worried about mine. I have to leave at 1pm today.

From: David Thorne
Date: Monday 21 June 2010 10:17 a.m.
To: Shannon Walkley
Subject: Re: Re: Re: Poster

Dear Shannon,

I never said I don't like cats. Once, having been invited to a party, I went clothes shopping beforehand and bought a pair of expensive G-Star boots. They were two sizes too small, but I wanted them so badly I figured I could just wear them without socks and cut my toenails very short.

As the party was only a few blocks from my place, I decided to walk. After the first block, I lost all feeling in my feet. Arriving at the party, I stumbled into a guy named Steven, spilling Malibu & Coke onto his white Wham "Choose Life" T-shirt, and he punched me. An hour or so after the incident, Steven sat down in a chair already occupied by a cat. The surprised cat clawed and snarled, causing Steven to leap out of the chair, slip on a rug, and strike his forehead onto the corner of a speaker, resulting in a two-inch open gash. In its shock, the cat also defecated, leaving Steven with a wet brown stain down the back of his beige cargo pants. I liked that cat. Attached poster as requested.

Regards, David

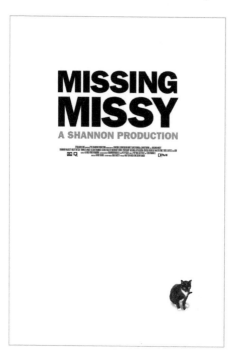

From: Shannon Walkley

Date: Monday 21 June 2010 10:24 a.m.

To: David Thorne

Subject: Re: Re: Re: Re: Poster

yeah thats not what I was looking for at all. it looks like a movie and how come the photo of Missy is so small?

From: David Thorne
Date: Monday 21 June 2010 10:28 a.m.
To: Shannon Walkley
Subject: Re: Re: Re: Re: Re: Poster

Dear Shannon,

It's a design thing. The cat is lost in the negative space.

Regards, David

From: Shannon Walkley
Date: Monday 21 June 2010 10:33 a.m.
To: David Thorne
Subject: Re: Re: Re: Re: Re: Re: Poster

Thats just stupid. Can you do it properly please? I am extremely emotional over this and was up all night in tears. you seem to think it is funny. Can you make the photo bigger and fix the text please.

From: David Thorne
Date: Monday 21 June 2010 10:46 a.m.
To: Shannon Walkley
Subject: Re: Re: Re: Re: Re: Re: Re: Poster

Dear Shannon,

Having worked with designers for a few years now, I would have assumed you understood, despite our vague suggestions otherwise, we do not welcome constructive criticism. I don't come downstairs and tell you how to send text messages, log onto Facebook, and look out of the window. I am willing to overlook this faux pas as you are no doubt preoccupied with thoughts of Missy attempting to make her way home across busy intersections or being trapped in a drain as it slowly fills with water. I spent three days down a well once, but that was just for fun.

I have amended and attached the poster as per your instructions.

Regards, David

From: Shannon Walkley
Date: Monday 21 June 2010 10:59 a.m.
To: David Thorne
Subject: Re: Re: Re: Re: Re: Re: Re: Re: Poster

This is worse than the other one. can you make it so it shows the whole photo of Missy and delete the stupid text that says missing missy off it? I just want it to say lost.

From: David Thorne
Date: Monday 21 June 2010 11:14 a.m.
To: Shannon Walkley
Subject: Re: Re: Re: Re: Re: Re: Re: Re: Re: Poster

From: Shannon Walkley
Date: Monday 21 June 2010 11:21 a.m.
To: David Thorne
Subject: Re: Re: Re: Re: Re: Re: Re: Re: Re: Re: Poster

yeah can you do the poster or not? I just want a photo and the word lost
and the telephone number and when and where she was lost and her
name. Not like a movie poster or anything stupid. I have to leave early
today. If it was your cat I would help you. Thanks.

From: David Thorne
Date: Monday 21 June 2010 11:32 a.m.
To: Shannon Walkley
Subject: Awww

Dear Shannon,

I don't have a cat. I once agreed to look after a friend's cat for a week, but after he dropped it off at my apartment and explained the concept of kitty litter, I kept the cat in a closed cardboard box in the shed and forgot about it. If I wanted to feed something and clean feces, I wouldn't have put my mother in that home after her stroke. A week later, when my friend came to collect his cat, I pretended that I was not home and mailed the box to him. Apparently, I failed to put enough stamps on the package, and he had to collect it from the post office and pay eighteen dollars. He still goes on about that sometimes, but people need to learn to let go. I have attached the amended version of your poster as per your detailed instructions.

Regards, David

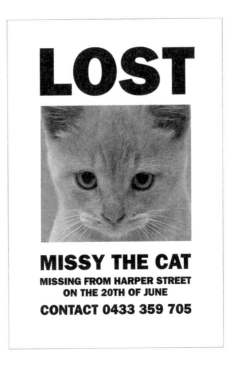

LOST

MISSY THE CAT
MISSING FROM HARPER STREET
ON THE 20TH OF JUNE
CONTACT 0433 359 705

From: Shannon Walkley
Date: Monday 21 June 2010 11:47 a.m.
To: David Thorne
Subject: Re: Awww

Thats not my cat. where did you get that picture from? That cat is orange. I gave you a photo of my cat.

From: David Thorne
Date: Monday 21 June 2010 11:58 a.m.
To: Shannon Walkley
Subject: Re: Re: Awww

I know, but that one is cute. As Missy has quite possibly met any one of several violent ends, it is possible you might get a better cat out of this. If anybody calls and says, "I haven't seen your orange cat, but I did find a black-and-white one with its hind legs run over by a car. Do you want it?" you can politely decline and save yourself a costly veterinarian bill.

I knew someone who had a Basset hound that had its hind legs removed after an accident, and it had to walk around with one of those little buggies with wheels. If it had been my dog I would have asked for all its legs to be removed and replaced with wheels and had a remote control installed. I could charge neighborhood kids for rides and enter it in races. If I did the same with a horse, I could drive it to work. I would call it Steven.

Regards, David

From: Shannon Walkley
Date: Monday 21 June 2010 12:07 p.m.
To: David Thorne
Subject: Re: Re: Re: Awww

Please just use the photo I gave you.

From: David Thorne
Date: Monday 21 June 2010 12:22 p.m.
To: Shannon Walkley
Subject: Re: Re: Re: Re: Awww

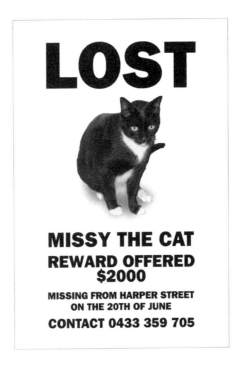

From: Shannon Walkley
Date: Monday 21 June 2010 12:34 p.m.
To: David Thorne
Subject: Re: Re: Re: Re: Re: Awww

I didnt say there was a reward. I dont have $2000 dollars. What did you even put that there for? Apart from that it is perfect can you please remove the reward bit. Thanks Shan.

From: David Thorne
Date: Monday 21 June 2010 12:42 p.m.
To: Shannon Walkley
Subject: Re: Re: Re: Re: Re: Re: Awww

From: Shannon Walkley
Date: Monday 21 June 2010 12:51 p.m.
To: David Thorne
Subject: Re: Re: Re: Re: Re: Re: Re: Awww

Can you just please take the reward bit off altogether? I have to leave in ten minutes and I still have to make photocopies of it.

From: David Thorne
Date: Monday 21 June 2010 12:56 p.m.
To: Shannon Walkley
Subject: Re: Re: Re: Re: Re: Re: Re: Re: Awww

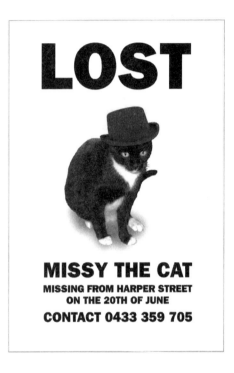

From: Shannon Walkley
Date: Monday 21 June 2010 1:03 p.m.
To: David Thorne
Subject: Re: Re: Re: Re: Re: Re: Re: Re: Re: Awww

Fine. That will have to do.

Hello, my name is Mark,
and I have head lice

When I was a schoolboy, every month the school nurse would have the children line up for a hair check. Many of my classmates were apprehensive of being found to have headlice, but the day the nurse declared, "Mark, you have headlice," I felt elated and excited by the idea of living beings choosing me as their provider and calling my hair home. I felt as if I had won a prize. I had never been allowed to have pets at home. My mother, who suffered from a compulsive disorder forcing her to clean, forbade any animals in the house. Unbeknownst to my mother, every night I would water the soil outside my bedroom window and play with the worms that would emerge. That afternoon when I rushed home and told my mother that I had been chosen, her reaction was not that which I had expected, and I was forced to wash my hair with KP24, a product designed to kill those that had chosen me. I learned to hate my mother that day and never forgave her. Fifteen years later, on the night she died, I leaned over and whispered into her ear that the same product she had used to perform genocide on my headlice was what was in her cup of tea.

Many people feel that headlice are of a sign of dirty or unhealthy hair, but this is simply not the case. Like those little fish that live under sharks or those tiny birds that clean alligator teeth, my headlice serve a double role of not only cleaning my scalp but also keeping me company. Often, I talk to my headlice or play them tunes on my acoustic guitar. Sometimes when it is very quiet and I concentrate very hard, I think that I can hear them talking to each other, and once, I am pretty sure I heard my name mentioned.

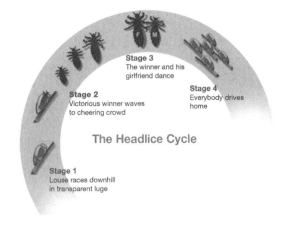

The Headlice Cycle

Stage 1
Louse races downhill
in transparent luge

Stage 2
Victorious winner waves
to cheering crowd

Stage 3
The winner and his
girlfriend dance

Stage 4
Everybody drives
home

A few months ago, I was at the hardware store buying a grass trim-mer and stopped at the sausage sizzle to purchase a snack. While I was waiting, I bought a raffle ticket that boasted three nights in Bali as first prize. I forgot about the ticket until last week when I found it in one of my old copies of *Nit Weekly* while looking for an article I had seen on headlice as an alternative fuel source. I called the number on the ticket—and I had won. While I was in Bali, I met a native girl and we fell in love. Returning home two nights later, I found that I had pubic lice. I was in the middle of feeding my new friends when my headlice formed a concentrated group and attacked the newcomers, leaving everyone dead. I believe, in protect-ing me from what they perceived as a threat, they displayed an obvious sign of love.

Another time, when I was canoeing on the river and had to jump out due to seeing a spider in the canoe with me, I forgot I could not swim and was going under, when each headlice held onto an individual hair and swam for the surface.

Raising headlice as pets can be a very rewarding experience. Your head-lice will provide you with many years of having something to do with your hands and a great deal of satisfaction knowing you helped to establish and

Unhealthy barren
environment

Healthy environment
teeming with life

build a community. As their host, it is important to provide them with the necessities of life. Once a week I give my hair a light spray with chicken stock. In summer I do this daily. On Easter weekend I add a small of amount of chocolate to the mixture, and at Christmas time I make them small presents using tweezers and a magnifying glass.

I have found that, with great care, your headlice community will thrive and is even transferable to other parts of your body. I currently have my hair buddies, as I like to call them, living not only on my head but also in my eyebrows, eyelashes, and armpits. When I am at the movie theater, I like to pick headlice out of my hair and place them onto the heads of people in front of me, thus helping my headlice colonize new territories.

STEVENSON
STRATA MANAGEMENT

Office
176 Fullarton Road
Dulwich, South Australia 5065

Postal Address
PO BOX 309
Kent Town, South Australia 5071

Phone
T 08 8291 2300
F 08 8364 1798

Accounts Department Contact:
Fax 08 8431 9433

Whittles Management Services Pty Ltd
atf Whittles Strata Unit Trust
trading as Whittles Strata Management

ABN 31 493 603 726

18th May, 2009

Mr David Thorne
████████████
████████████
Adelaide, South Australia

Dear Mr Thorne,

It has come to our attention through complaints by other tenants
in your building that you have a dog at the premises. Under the
agreement you signed as part of the Strata, animals are not
permitted.

Please call me or email me at hel███████████n.com.au to
discuss this matter as soon as possible.

Yours Sincerely,

Helen Bailey

Strata rules
exist for the benefit of
all residents

If I had a large backyard, I would probably have about a thousand dogs, but as my apartment is very small, I cannot have any due to both the Strata agreement and the fact that they would need to be taken for walks every day, and I am too lazy for that. There is a park across the road from us, but the last time I went there I was offered money to provide a sexual act, which was flattering, but I told them that I was late for a meeting, which was a lie, as I think I just played *Unreal Tournament* the rest of that day.

I did have a goldfish named (posthumously) Stinky who lived in a vase with a plant. When he died I figured it would be nice to leave him there so that his body would break down and fertilize the plant, but after a few weeks, the smell was so bad I could not enter the apartment without a towel wrapped around my face. My first thought was to take him to work and hide him in my bosses car, but out of respect Seb and I gave him a Viking's funeral instead.

From: David Thorne
Date: Thursday 21 May 2009 10:16 a.m.
To: Helen Bailey
Subject: Pets in the building

Dear Helen,

Thank you for your letter concerning pets in my apartment. I understand that having dogs in the apartment is a violation of the agreement due to the comfort and well-being of my neighbors, and I am currently soundproofing my apartment with egg cartons because I realize my dogs can cause quite a bit of noise. Especially during feeding time, when I release live rabbits.

Regards, David

From: Helen Bailey
Date: Thursday 21 May 2009 11:18 a.m.
To: David Thorne
Subject: Re: Pets in the building

Hello David

I've received your e-mail and wish to remind you that the agreement states that no animals are allowed in the building regardless of if your apartment is soundproof. How many dogs do you have at the premises?

Helen

From: David Thorne
Date: Thursday 21 May 2009 1:52 p.m.
To: Helen Bailey
Subject: Re: Re: Pets in the building

Dear Helen,

Currently I have only eight dogs, but one is expecting puppies, and I am very excited by this. I am hoping for a litter of at least ten, as this is the number required to participate in dogsled racing. I have read every Jack London novel in preparation and have constructed my own sled from timber I borrowed from the construction site across the road during the night. I have devised a plan that I feel will ensure me taking first place in the next national dogsled championships. For the first year of the puppies' lives I intend to say the word "Mush!" and then chase them violently around the apartment while yelling and hitting saucepan lids together. I have estimated that the soundproofing of my apartment should block out at least 60 percent of the noise, and the dogs will learn to associate the word "mush" with great fear, so when I yell it on race day, the panic, and released adrenaline, will spur them on to being winners. I am so confident of this being a foolproof plan that I intend to sell all my furniture the day before the race and bet the proceeds on coming in first place.

Regards, David

From: Helen Bailey
Date: Friday 22 May 2009 9:43 a.m.
To: David Thorne
Subject: Re: Re: Re: Pets in the building

David, I'm unsure what to make of your e-mail. Do you have pets in the apartment or not?

Helen

From: David Thorne
Date: Friday 22 May 2009 11:27 a.m.
To: Helen Bailey
Subject: Re: Re: Re: Re: Pets in the building

Dear Helen,

No. I have a goldfish, but due to the air conditioner in my apartment being stuck on a constant two degrees Celsius, the water in its bowl is iced over and he has not moved for a while, so I do not think he is capable of disturbing the neighbors. The ducks in the bathroom are not mine. The noise that my neighbors possibly mistook for a dog in the apartment is just the looping tape I have of dogs barking, which I play at high volume while I am at work to deter potential burglars from breaking in and stealing my Tupperware. I need it to keep food fresh. Once I ate leftover Chinese that had been kept in an unsealed container, and I experienced complete awareness. The next night I tried eating it again but experienced only chest pains and diarrhea.

Regards, David

From: Helen Bailey
Date: Friday 22 May 2009 1:46 p.m.
To: David Thorne
Subject: Re: Re: Re: Re: Re: Pets in the building

Hello David

You cannot play sounds of dogs or any noise at a volume that disturbs others. I am sure you can appreciate that these rules are for the benefit of all residents of the building. Fish are fine. You cannot have ducks in the apartment though. If it was small birds that would be ok.

Helen

From: David Thorne
Date: Friday 22 May 2009 2:18 p.m.
To: Helen Bailey
Subject: Re: Re: Re: Re: Re: Re: Pets in the building

Dear Helen,

They are very small ducks.

Regards, David

From: Helen Bailey
Date: Friday 22 May 2009 4:06 p.m.
To: David Thorne
Subject: Re: Re: Re: Re: Re: Re: Re: Pets in the building

David, under section 4 of the Strata Residency Agreement it states that you cannot have pets. You agreed to these rules when you signed the forms. These rules are set out to benefit everyone in the building including yourself. Do you have a telephone number I can call you on to discuss?

Helen

From: David Thorne
Date: Friday 22 May 2009 5:02 p.m.
To: Helen Bailey
Subject: Re: Re: Re: Re: Re: Re: Re: Re: Pets in the building

Dear Helen,

The ducks will no doubt be flying south for the winter soon, so it will not be an issue. It is probably for the best, as they are not getting along very well with my seventeen cats, anyway.

Regards, David

From: Helen Bailey
Date: Monday 25 May 2009 9:22 a.m.
To: David Thorne
Subject: Re: Re: Re: Re: Re: Re: Re: Re: Re: Pets in the building

David, I am just going to write on the forms that we have investigated and you do not have any pets.

Helen

Hello, my name is Lucius, and I'd like you to sign here, please

I am probably the best courier in the world. If you have a box and you want it to go somewhere, I will come and get it and take it there instead of you having to do it yourself. You have to pay me to do it, but it saves you time, so it is worth it. It doesn't matter what kind of box—once I delivered a box full of bolts, which was really heavy. I am very strong, though. They were saying, "Wow, that box looks heavy," and I replied, "No, it's light for me."

PICKUP & DELIVERY LOG

8:30 a.m.
The first pickup and delivery of the day is always the best. When I am driving to collect the first box of the day, I try to guess what color it will be and what will be in it. If the tape on the box is the kind you can lift and put back, I have a look. Sometimes there is food in there. I don't eat it, though, as that would be against the Courier Code. Once, there was a whole box of sandwiches to be delivered to a work function, and they wouldn't have noticed if I had eaten one, but I didn't. I took a little bite out of each one, but that is allowed.

9:45 a.m.
YES! It was a brown box! I knew it would be a brown box. I have definitely got psychotic powers. I have guessed the box would be brown eight hundred and forty times in a row, which proves my powers are probably the most powerful in the world. I have to keep my powers a secret, though, as the government would want to control someone as powerful as I probably am. I would have to live my life on the run, never settling down in one place

for long. The government would probably hunt me down and fifty of them would point their guns at me, and I would concentrate, and the guns would float up in the air or turn into sticks, and the men would say, "He is more powerful than we thought possible." I pulled up around the corner to have a look inside the box, but it was just books, which was disappointing.

10:30 a.m.

I delivered the box, and the girl in the front foyer signed and printed her name. Her name is Kate, and I could tell by the sexy way she signed that she thought I was one of the top five best lookingest guys in Adelaide and wished I were her boyfriend. I was telling her about my psychotic powers and was going to ask her out, but she said she was really busy and had to get back to work. I will see her again later today, though, as they are regular clients. I will write her a poem during my lunch break. On the way out the door I took a couple of photos of her on my camera phone. She looks a bit surprised in the first photo and blurry in the second, as she was getting out of her chair as the door closed. I will use the flash next time. It is somewhere in Settings. When anyone has a problem with their phone they always get me to fix it because I am like a computer genius. I am probably the biggest computer genius in the world; I just can't be bothered learning all that stuff.

11:15 a.m.

Stuck in traffic on my way to the next box pickup. I feel it might be brown. I like to listen to music while I am waiting and have all the best albums recorded onto TDK Cassette, including *Arrival, Super Trouper,* and *Warterloo.* When I make the final payment on my delivery van in fourteen years, I am going to have a CD player installed. I saw them at Kmart for only $49.95, so am saving for one. When I am waiting in traffic I turn the music up as loud as it will go, and all the rattles in the van vibrate along to it; it is like my van is dancing. Sometimes I become lost in the beat and imagine that I am Paula Abdul, dancing with the cartoon cat on the stairs in that music clip where she dances with the cartoon cat on the stairs. I am also probably one of the best singers in the world, and when my friend Jedd is in the van, I say to him, "Make me that beat already so I can destroy it with my unstoppable flows," and he does.

12:45 p.m.
Eight hundred and forty-one! It is a big box too. Priority pickup from one hospital to another. I should not have looked inside that one. I will deliver it after I finish my lunch break and sponge wash. I always keep a wet sponge in the back, and I park the van, undress, and sponge myself down so that I am clean and refreshed for the rest of the day. I stopped off at Target and bought cologne and a suit I am going to wear for Kate. I have also written her a poem:

"Kate" *By Lucius*

I delivered you a box today
It was brown with clear tape wrapped around it.
I am in the back of my van looking at photos of you
Imagining you opening the box
Wondering what is in it, because I didn't look.
The tape was like that when I picked it up.

3:20 p.m.
I have just left the hospital; they were quite rude. A nurse said that she was going to ring my boss, and I told her, "He might be the boss of me, but I am the boss of my life," which was obviously too philosophical for her, because she just stood there looking at me. She was completely porned. If I were a Transformer she would be so sorry. I took a whole bunch of latex gloves while she was not looking and am on my way to pick up a box to be delivered to the company that Kate works for. I have a strong feeling that this box will be brown, and I will drive really fast to get it to her quickly so she sees how professional and efficient I am. I am probably the best driver in the world, and if I were a racing car driver I would be world champion.

3:50 p.m.

Eight hundred and forty-two! I had to climb six flights of stairs to collect the box, but I am very fit and athletic as I own a trampoline and do four hours of air running every night. Air running is where you jump really high and then run as fast as you can in the air. It is very good for the vascular system, and often my neighbors will come out to watch me. If it were a team sport I would be captain. I am on my way to deliver the box to Kate. I can't wait to see her, and I bet she is as excited as I am. I have changed into my suit and put on cologne. I will stand very close to her so that she can smell it. I have cleaned the van up a little bit, as I will ask her to come for a ride. Also, I read somewhere that girls like it when you ask them about themselves, so in addition to the poem, I have compiled a list of questions for her to fill out about where she lives and what she does.

5:10 p.m.

I am on my way back to the depot because my boss rang and said he needs to see me immediately. Probably to give me a raise or promotion. I delivered the box and Kate absolutely loved her poem; I read it out to her and she was speechless. There were tears in her eyes, and she was shaking, so I could tell she was overcome with emotion. She couldn't come for a ride in my van because she had a dentist appointment, but I could tell she wanted to. She asked me my full name and then repeated it to someone on the phone, so I know she feels the same way I do if she is telling her friends about our love. I will buy her lunch tomorrow and surprise her by taking it in and eating it there with her. I will say, "Special delivery," and when she asks what it is, I will say, "Me. And a Subway footlong."

Hello, my name is Jason,
and I'm a good drawer

"Hello, sir, my name is Jason, and I was wondering if your company would be interested in a good drawer? No? Thank you for your time."

People often say to me, "Jason, you are a good drawer," and I say, "Thank you." To some people, being a good drawer may seem like a hobby rather than a profession, but I take it very seriously. Each fortnight, eighteen dollars (20 percent) of my income is spent on charcoal and butcher's paper. It is an investment in my future.

Here are some of my drawings; they are all for sale. Please contact me immediately if you wish to purchase some of these masterpieces, which will no doubt prove to be a very handsome investment.

Name
Whale Looking For
Mate

Media
Charcoal on butcher
paper

Price
$2,800

Name
Nina in Floral Dress,
Summertime

Media
Charcoal on butcher
paper

Price
$5,200

Name
Friendly Tiger

Media
Charcoal on butcher
paper

Price
$3,000

Shannon's
color-coded coffee cleaning chart

Due to there being an unprecedented twelve coffee cups needing to be cleaned in the sink at work, it is understandable that Shannon would be outraged by this intrusion on her "Facebook and looking out the window" time. Though kitchen duties may be an expected part of her job role, there is no reason why everyone should not reschedule work/client commitments and help out, to ensure Shannon's social networking and looking out the window time is not interrupted.

From: Shannon
Date: Monday 17 August 2009 10:12 a.m.
To: Staff
Subject: Coffee cups

There was twelve coffee cups left in the sink this morning. Could you please wash coffee cups after using them. Thanks, Shan

From: David Thorne
Date: Monday 17 August 2009 10:19 a.m.
To: Shannon
Subject: Re: Coffee cups

Morning Shannon,

My apologies. Those coffee cups were mine. I am rather busy today so decided to have all of my coffee breaks at the one time this morning rather than taking twelve separate breaks throughout the day. I am currently experiencing severe heart palpitations but also typing at four hundred and seventy words per minute so should be able to leave early.

Regards, David

From: Shannon
Date: Monday 17 August 2009 10:31 a.m.
To: David Thorne
Subject: Re: Re: Coffee cups

I was not saying they were all your coffee cups I was just saying that I shouldn't have to wash twelve coffee cups when I don't drink coffee. People should wash their own coffee cups or at least take it in turns to wash them.

From: David Thorne
Date: Monday 17 August 2009 10:42 a.m.
To: Shannon
Subject: Re: Re: Re: Coffee cups

Shannon,

You raise a valid and not at all uninteresting point. Perhaps you could construct some kind of chart. A roster system would enable us to work in an environment free of dirty coffee cups and put an end to any confusion regarding who the dirty coffee cup responsibility lies with.

David

From: Shannon
Date: Monday 17 August 2009 1:08 p.m.
To: Staff
Subject: Kitchen Roster

Hi everyone. I have discussed a kitchen roster with David and feel it
would be fair if we took it in turns to do the dishes. I have put the roster
in the kitchen so everyone can remember. I am Monday morning
and Wednesday and Friday afternoon. David is Monday afternoon and
Wednesday morning, Lillian is Tuesday morning and Thursday afternoon
and Thomas is Tuesday afternoon and Friday morning.

Thanks, Shan

From: David Thorne
Date: Monday 17 August 2009 1:22 p.m.
To: Shannon
Subject: Color coded coffee cup cleaning chart

Shannon, I notice that you have color-coded the coffee-cup-cleaning
chart. While I appreciate the creative effort that has gone into this roster,
the light salmon color you have chosen for my name is very effeminate.
While I am sure you have not done this on purpose and are not inferring
anything, I would appreciate you rectifying this immediately. Would it be
possible to swap colors with Thomas, as he has quite a nice dusty blue?

Thank you, David

From: Shannon
Date: Monday 17 August 2009 2:17 p.m.
To: Staff
Subject: Updated kitchen roster

Hi. I have changed David's color to blue on the kitchen roster. Thomas is now green.

Shan

From: Thomas
Date: Monday 17 August 2009 2:24 p.m.
To: David Thorne
Subject: What the fuck?

What the fuck is this e-mail from Shannon? I am not doing a fucking kitchen roster. Was this your idea?

From: David Thorne
Date: Monday 17 August 2009 2:38 p.m.
To: Thomas **Cc:** Shannon
Subject: Re: What the fuck?

Thomas, do you feel it is fair that Shannon should have to wash everyone's coffee cups? Apparently, this morning there were twelve coffee cups in the sink. I was going to schedule a staff meeting this afternoon to discuss the issue, but luckily, Shannon has prepared a color-coded coffee-cup-cleaning chart for us, rendering a staff meeting unnecessary. We should all thank Shannon for taking the initiative and creating a system that will empower us to efficiently schedule client meetings and work commitments around our designated coffee-cup-cleaning duties. If at any stage our rostered coffee-cup-cleaning commitments coincide with work requirements, we can simply hold the client meeting in the kitchen. We can wash while the clients dry. Today it may be only twelve coffee cups, but tomorrow it could be several plates and a spoon, and then where would we be?

David

From: Thomas
Date: Monday 17 August 2009 2:56 p.m.
To: Shannon
Subject: Kitchen stuff

Shannon, I do not need a chart telling me when to wash dishes. I'm not going to stop in the middle of writing proposals to wash cups.
    David is being a fuckwit. I only use one coffee cup and I always rinse it out after I use it. If we have clients here and they use coffee cups then it is appreciated that you wash them as part of your job.

From: Lillian
Date: Monday 17 August 2009 3:06 p.m.
To: Thomas
Subject: Re: Kitchen stuff

What's this kitchen roster thing? Did you agree to this?

From: David Thorne
Date: Monday 17 August 2009 3:09 p.m.
To: Shannon
Subject: Rescheduling coffee cup duties

Shannon, can I swap my rostered coffee-cup-cleaning duty this afternoon for Thursday? I have been busy all day working, not looking at pictures of Johnny Depp on the Internet, and not had time to familiarize myself with correct coffee-cup-cleaning requirements. I am happy to reschedule my meetings tomorrow to undertake a training session on dish washing detergent location and washcloth procedures with you if you have the time. I feel it would be quite helpful if prior to the training session you prepared some kind of PowerPoint presentation. Possibly with graphs. Will I need to bring my own rubber gloves, or will these be provided?

David

From: Shannon
Date: Monday 17 August 2009 3:20 p.m.
To: David Thorne
Subject: Re: Rescheduling coffee cup duties

Whatever.

Simon's
step-by-step guide to camping

Hello, my name is Simon, and I love camping. I do not own any camping gear, but this is not a problem, as I have watched every season of *Survivor.* My favorite season so far was the one where Jeff, the host, rode all the way from the Amazon on a jet-ski to New York, crossing the Atlantic Ocean, to read the votes in the final episode. This shows not only great dedication to fans but also excellent seafaring and navigation skills. It would have taken him ages, plus he would have had to stop to rest and eat.

Step 1

Ring David at 11 p.m. and tell him you want to go camping the next day. Dictate a list of items you require him to prepare by the next morning, including tent and all supplies. If David asks any questions, become exasperated and explain to him that camping is about enjoying the great outdoors and each other's company, not about going halves for groceries and petrol money.

Step 2

Ring David at 6:45 a.m. to add "Biscuits to eat on the trip" to the list.

Step 3

Once David arrives to pick you up, read out the list and make David say the word "check" after each item because that is how they do it on television and "yep" is not a real word. Add "Pocket mirror" to the list, berating

David for not having the common sense to include this should you need to signal planes. Quote Lord Baden-Powell's "Be Prepared" a minimum of four times. Before leaving, try on several combinations of cargo pants with baseball caps and consult David on the merits of each. If David states, "That looks fine," explain to him that you were just testing him and he failed, as you would never wear a green baseball cap with beige cargo pants out in public. If he mentions nobody else will be at the campsite to see the outfit, explain to him that you are taking a digital camera and will not be posting photos on Facebook of you wearing a green baseball cap with beige cargo pants.

Step 4

Instruct David to take your bags out to the car while you check your e-mail before leaving. Explain the importance of working together and good time management. Once you have left, instruct David to pull into a service station to purchase AAA batteries and different biscuits to eat on the trip, as you like only the ones with cream in them. When David returns to the car, go into the service station to purchase biscuits yourself after stating that it should have been obvious you did not mean Oreo's. While inside, also purchase Billy Idol's greatest hits CD to listen to on the way because you like the track "Yell Like a Rebel."

Step 5

During the four-hour drive to the campsite, instruct David to pull over every forty-five minutes so you can go to the toilet behind a tree. It is important to do this when the only tree is several hundred meters away in a field. While urinating, peer around the tree at David sitting in the car. For the remainder of the drive, list words that lose all meaning when you say them fifty times such as "yolk," warn David to watch out for kangaroos every ten minutes, and play Billy Idol's *Greatest Hits* on loop while stating, "Oooh, I remember this one," at the beginning of each track. Read out each road sign as you pass it. When it is a speed limit sign, lean across to glance at the speedometer.

Step 6

Upon arrival, unpack only a chair to sit in, while David sets up camp. Point out what he could do to streamline the procedure. Instruct David to fetch your bag because you did not realize the tent would be the same color as your cargo pants and you wish to change. Explain that if you are photographed with the tent in the background it will look like you have no legs. Admonish David for purchasing AAA batteries when your digital camera takes AA. Inform David that AA and AAA are the correct terms and that only people who drive pickup trucks call them double A and triple A.

Step 7

After sitting in the chair for an hour, inform David that you are bored. If David suggests hiking or any other activity that requires leaving the chair, state that you are there to relax, not partake in extreme sports.

Step 8

While David collects firewood to cook dinner, call out instructions regarding the size, type, and density of wood required. As David is constructing the fire, point out the fundamental errors of his system and state that it is not the way you have seen it done on *Survivor.* Explain the tee-pee method of stick formation and its air circulation and flame consistency benefits. Once the fire is established, describe in detail how you prefer your sausages cooked, using pieces of bark as color swatches to indicate the hue required. During dinner, calculate the ratio of burned to unburned sausage and evaluate David's ability to follow simple instructions at 17 percent. After dinner, state that it is a requirement while camping to sing songs around the campfire. When David declines, sing tracks from Billy Idol's *Greatest Hits* CD. After asking David if he thinks your hair would look good styled like Billy Idol's, point out his obvious lack of fashion sense using the green cap and beige pants example.

Step 9

Declare that you are tired and wish to go to bed. If David replies that he will sit by the fire for a while, inform him that you are camping together and to douse the fire with a bucket of water. Once in the tent, state that you always sleep naked and are not going to alter this just because you are camping. Wait until David is in his sleeping bag before requesting he retrieve your book from the car due to your being naked, not tired, and wishing to read for a while by torchlight. On his return, point out the fact that the torch is flat and that it takes AA batteries. Lie in the dark for several minutes before declaring that you are bored and that there may be a mosquito in the tent. Ask, "Did you hear that?" and "Are you asleep?" every five minutes. Describe how uncomfortable you are and what you are missing on television, and hum tracks from Billy Idol's *Greatest Hits* CD.

Step 10

Wake David at 1 a.m. and inform him that you want to make a bow and arrow. List the protection and hunting benefits of such. If David states that it is the middle of the night and there is no string for the bows, inform him that clocks are not part of camping and quote Lord Baden-Powell in regard to the string. Take this opportunity to point out a small hole in the tent and ask David if he thinks it is large enough for spiders to get through. Describe in depth a television program you saw on Discovery Channel about wasps laying eggs in spiders.

Step 11

Wake David at 1:30 a.m. and ask if he thinks the hole is large enough for wasps to get through.

Step 12

Wake David at 2 a.m. and tell him that you do not remember switching the iron off after ironing your cargo pants and that you are very concerned about the fact. Inform him that this will require cutting the camping trip short, packing up first thing in the morning and driving home. State that on the plus side, you just remembered the new series of *V* starts tomorrow night on television and this means that you will not miss it. List science fiction shows from the seventies and eighties that you think should be redone for today's audience.

Step 13

During the drive back, insinuate continuously that the Billy Idol CD has gone missing on purpose. State every half hour that you really felt like listening to it.

MASSANUTTEN
PROPERTY OWNERS ASSOCIATION

3980 MASSANUTTEN DRIVE MASSANUTTEN, VIRGINIA 22840 TEL: 540/289-9466 FAX: 540/289-9406
WEBSITE: www.massanuttenvillage.com EMAIL: mpoa@massanuttenvillage.com

Date: OCTOBER 6, 2010

To: Resident

Property: ███████████e, Massanutten Village, VA, 22840

Offence: MPOA Section 9   No. 008731

section 9 of the Massanutten Resident Agreement

9. No trash may be put out before Sunday evening. Any trash not in a secured trash container or trash dispersed by animals may be picked up by MPOA employees and owner may be billed for cost. Bear proof trash cans have been provided at Hopkins Park and the MPOA pool located on Peak Drive for overflow or early check-out trash.

- [ ] **Trash placed for collection prior to Sunday evening**
- [x] **Unsecured bags**
- [ ] **Unsecured Food Items**

- -

Payments must made at the Property Owners Office located at 3980 Massanutten Drive during office hours Monday to Friday. Please bring property owner ID with you.

Description of Offence: Unsecured Trash

TOTAL AMOUNT DUE: $75.00

NAME:

Payment by [ ] **Check** [ ] **Card** [ ] **Cash**   **Office Stamp:**

Massanutten
mini-golf, water slides, and bears

Massanutten is a small holiday community in Virginia, with a population currently comprising of two thousand old people, their cats, one Australian on a tourist visa, his beautiful partner, and a dog named Further. Me being an Australian, the town of Massanutten is like another planet to me. A heavily wooded planet founded by Norman Rockwell and colonized by John Deere tractor owners with a vision that included water slides and mini-golf.

Along with mini-golf, water slides, old people, cats, one Australian, his partner, and a dog named Further, Massanutten apparently has bears. I haven't seen any yet, but that is only, I assume, due to most people following rules outlined in section 9 of the MPOA Agreement.

From: David Thorne
Date: Thursday 7 October 2010 11:04 a.m.
To: mpoa@massanuttenvillage.com
Subject: Bears

Dear Sir and/or Madam,

I have received a request for seventy-five of my dollars for putting my trash out for collection without securing it inside a bear-proof container. Due to a series of events the night before, I forgot to put my trash out and had to run it out the next morning, after hearing the collection truck approach.

As regulations govern actions only within certain defined limits and thereby justify all similar actions that lie outside those limits, I request that my offense is changed from "Unsecured trash" to "Secured trash, barring the possibility of bears formulating a strategy in which to take advantage of the few minutes between deposit and collection."

Regards, David

From: Patricia Jennings
Date: Thursday 7 October 2010 5:16 p.m.
To: David Thorne
Subject: Re: Bears

Hello Mr. Thorne

Section 9 of the MPOA Agreement which you would have signed clearly states that trash must be secured. The reason we have these rules is so that bears and other large animals are not attracted to the area. This is for everyones safety. All bear sightings should be reported immediately to the MPOA. A ladys cat was almost bitten by a bear just a few weeks ago near the mini golf course.

Patricia

From: David Thorne
Date: Thursday 7 October 2010 9:12 p.m.
To: Patricia Jennings
Subject: Re: Re: Bears

Dear Pat,

Due to the abundant supply of cats in the area, I'm surprised bears bother with the trash at all. As I have run over at least four cats this week and one of those did not put up much of a chase, it may be suggested that elderly residents and their cats pose more of an attraction for bears than unsecured trash. For the safety of all residents, section 9 of the MPOA Agreement should probably be amended to state that all cats and their elderly owners be kept in bear-proof containers.

While out walking this evening, I witnessed several cats having some kind of cat meeting on the sidewalk ahead of me. Possibly discussing the local bear problem. After reading that a bear recently ate a lady's cat in the area and hearing a twig snap in the shadows behind me, I decided to take the shortest route home by cutting through the Massanutten mini-golf facilities. Managing to scale the three-meter fence via fear and a trash can, I slipped, caught my back pants pocket on one of the pointy metal bars, and hung there for several minutes before managing to wriggle out of them—dropping to safety and to the right of hole 7. Fashioning temporary legwear by removing my jumper and placing my legs in the sleeves, figuring they would look like Hammer pants to people driving by, I left the premises by climbing the papier-mâché boulders near hole 16, leaping onto the ticket hut roof, and dropping down the other side to safety. If my shoes had not been soaked and slippery from the pond to the right of hole 7, I am pretty sure I would have made it on the first attempt. While not pointing any blame, I quite liked those pants, because they fit really well and cost me around seventy-five dollars.

Also, as per your instructions to report bear sightings immediately, I have attached a photograph taken outside my premises a few minutes ago. I apologize for the quality but was fearful of getting too close due to the fact bears constrict and consume their prey whole, taking several days to fully digest. As I have a short attention span and would prefer a quick death, such as removing my helmet in space, I request you send assistance immediately.

Regards, David

From: Patricia Jennings
Date: Friday 8 October 2010 2:26 p.m.
To: David Thorne
Subject: Re: Re: Re: Bears

I checked with Carol at the mini golf hut and no pants were found on the fence. I doubt any of that really happened. That looks like a dog with a blanket on it. I'm not going to waste anyones time sending an officer out to check that.

From: David Thorne
Date: Friday 8 October 2010 2:51 p.m.
To: Patricia Jennings
Subject: Re: Re: Re: Re: Bears

Dear Pat,

If Carol from the mini-golf hut has time to check the perimeter for pants, why not send her? While issuing me a seventy-five dollar fine by justifying it is for the safety of others, you seem pretty quick to dismiss mine. As people rely on your protection from bears and your position consists entirely of not waiving fines issued, to ensure the compliance of regulations that protect people from bears, you should probably send out a memo or something stating that we are on our own in an emergency situation. On the back of the memo, you could include instructions on making a pointy stick to protect us with.

I own a gun but am unsure if a bear shot with a Daisy .177 caliber BB air rifle purchased from Wal-Mart for $39.75 would be wounded or just pissed off. While testing the rifle last week, my offspring was definitely the latter. I have heard that the best way to protect yourself during a bear attack is to roll into a tight ball and cover your face, but I am pretty sure a flame-thrower or a special suit that metal spikes spring out of when you press a button would be more effective. I have also heard that music soothes the savage beast, but the last time I sang Whitney Houston's "The Greatest Love of All" to my offspring, it had the opposite effect, despite what I considered to be an excellent reproduction of her tonal range.

Although wary, after reading recently that a bear ate a lady and her cat in the area, I decided to risk leaving the premises in order to drive to your office and pay the fine. Unfortunately, possibly due to an unsecured Snickers bar on the dashboard, the bear is now in my vehicle, and I am unable to do so. Please send assistance immediately as I have also run out of cigarettes and need to drive to the shop. If you send Carol, please ask her to stop on the way and grab me a pack. While you may not class this as an emergency or possible danger to others, you haven't seen me after two hours without nicotine.

Regards, David

From: Patricia Jennings
Date: Friday 8 October 2010 3:18 p.m.
To: David Thorne
Subject: Re: Re: Re: Re: Re: Bears

I wont be sending an officer because your not in any danger at all. You have obviously just put a blanket on a dog while it is sitting in your car and taken a photo. If you want to express your opinion on trash collection rules you are welcome to attend the next MPOA community meeting which is held each month. Not understanding the importance of bear safety doesnt mean you dont have to follow the rules. I'm not even sure what your point is.

From: David Thorne
Date: Friday 8 October 2010 4:22 p.m.
To: Patricia Jennings
Subject: Re: Re: Re: Re: Re: Re: Bears

Dear Pat,

My point is, barring the possibility of strategy-formulating bears, stating my actions constitute a punishable breach of regulations structured to protect the community only enables you to be wrong with authority, not right.

Contrary to your statement, I do understand the importance of bear safety. Several years ago, I went camping with a few associates and thought it would be amusing to jump out of bushes while wearing a bear suit. Renting the only bear costume available, which was a koala, I altered it as best I could to make it look frightening by taping down the fluffy ears, adding sharp cardboard teeth, and constructing two downward slanting eyebrows with electrical tape. While sitting around the campfire, I excused myself, donned the concealed costume, and leaped out, yelling, "Rawr!" Moments later, I realized the screaming and falling back off chairs was not due to my wearing a bear costume but the fact that I was standing in the fire while wearing a bear costume made of polyester. After a two-hour drive to the nearest hospital, I underwent three weeks of skin-grafting on my left leg and six months of hearing about how I ruined the camping trip. To this day, when anyone asks about the scars, I simply state, "It involved a camping trip and a bear—I don't like to talk about it," which is true, because I don't. While I was in the hospital, my mother went to my apartment to get some clothes for me and found my porn collection, so it is a touchy subject.

Also, while I was able to persuade the bear to exit my vehicle by pretending to be an old lady looking for her cat, it is now inside my premises. Although not immediately evident from the attached photograph, the bear is sitting between me and the television remote control, located on the cushion to its left. As this effectively cuts off my ability to change channels and *The View* just started, this should be classed as an emergency situation. If I wanted to watch a group of old women carry on, I would attend an MPOA community meeting.

Regards, David

Fine. I will waive the amount this time if you agree to make sure all your trash is secure in future.

From: David Thorne
Date: Friday 8 October 2010 5:16 p.m.
To: Patricia Jennings
Subject: Re: Re: Re: Re: Re: Re: Re: Re: Bears

Dear Pat,

Regardless of whether you waive the fine or not, and despite conditional terms added to reassert authority, I will continue to secure trash correctly. Not because it is a rule, but because it is a logical rule to follow. Despite my continuing doubt as to the ability of bears to plan and execute maneuvers requiring SWAT team precision, I will also do so regardless of the time frame between deposit and collection. Not because it is a logical rule to follow, but because it is a rule.

How about you agree to waive the fine and I promise not to e-mail you the remaining eighty-six photos of my dog dressed as a bear?

Regards, David

From: Patricia Jennings
Date: Friday 8 October 2010 5:24 p.m.
To: David Thorne
Subject: Re: Re: Re: Re: Re: Re: Re: Re: Re: Bears

Agreed.

Bill's guide
to everything on the Internet

Hello, my name is Bill, and welcome to my guide to the Internet. Basically, everything on the Internet is rubbish, but I will try to pinpoint the main areas to avoid. The Internet is full of idiots writing rubbish for other idiots to read. If I want to find something out I will ask someone or read a book. I paid more than three thousand dollars for my complete leather-bound set of Funk & Wagnalls in 1967, and if it is not in there, then it is not worth knowing. Also, man will walk on the moon before I have a Facebook page.

Google

When I was young and I wanted to know something, I was beaten for being too inquisitive. That's the problem with the young people today: They have a Google answer for everything. If they had to walk to their local library every time they had something stupid to ask, they would ask a lot fewer stupid questions.

Google Images

Google Images is useless. I used it once to search for a photo of farm equipment, and it showed me twenty thousand pictures of horse dicks.

Blogging

I read a blog once by someone who had bought a scarf, and he went on for about three hundred paragraphs about his scarf and where he bought it and how it made him feel. The last time I bought a scarf, I wore it. End of story. I didn't write a novel about it.

Chat Rooms

If I wanted to chat with strangers, I would pick up the phone and press random numbers. I tried a chat room once and was talking to a guy who claimed he was an obese fifty-three-year-old man living in a caravan park, but there is no way of knowing if these people are telling the truth.

The Bath Mat

I realize this is not Internet-related, but I cannot understand why it is so hard for people to hang the bath mat over the bath when they are finished using it. I don't leave the mat all soggy for other people to walk on after I have been in there.

Twitter

Why would I want anybody I don't know knowing what I am doing? I don't yell out to everyone in the supermarket, "I am buying oranges!" So why would I want to do it on my Internet? When I was young, I lived in a small village where everybody knew each other and knew what everyone was up to. There was a fat Italian kid who lived next door to me named Tony. One day I shot him in the leg with a homemade bow and arrow from my tree house that overlooked his yard, and his parents called the police. Within hours the entire village was calling me William Tell. Having escaped the small town mentality for the last fifty-two years, I am hardly going to advertise my movements now.

Facebook

I have a photo album on my bookshelf full of faces of people I know that I haven't opened since 1982, so why would I want their faces on my Internet? None of them are even very good looking. I tried Facebook to see what all the fuss was about and was only on there five minutes before some idiot "Poked" me. It is easy to be brave when you are on the Internet.

Reddit/Digg

These sites are the online equivalent of walking down the street, finding a rock shaped like a frog, and holding it up in the air while yelling for all my neighbors to come out and tell me what they think of my frog-shaped rock. My neighbors can all go to hell. Especially Mrs. Carter in number three who leaves her bins out all week. If I did find a rock shaped like a frog, I would throw it at her.

eBay

If I wanted a house full of cheap, dirty, secondhand rubbish, I would go to a garage sale in Klemzig.

E-mail

People are always sending me all kinds of rubbish. Why would I want dozens of pictures of lots of love cats? I hate cats. I went away for a week recently, and when I got back and checked my e-mail, I had eight hundred and forty-three messages. Eight hundred and forty of these were adverts for Viagra, and the other three were pictures of lots of love cats. I bought a "No junk mail" sticker and stuck it on my modem, but nobody has taken any notice.

/b/

I spent a good hour on this site and still have no idea what it is for. All I could work out is that I am apparently a "newfag" and cannot "triforce" but am unsure as to why I would need to triforce in the first place. I asked some of the people on there for their advice regarding triforcing, but the only answer I seemed to get was "nigger."

BOX 1539 GPO, ADELAIDE SA 5001
TELEPHONE: 8207 6000
ASN 93 799 021 552

Your Ref
Our Ref   PO8 2010/7281
Enquiries
Telephone
Facsimile

25 February 2010

Mr David Thorne
PO Box 10476
ADELAIDE BC SOUTH AUSTRALIA 5000

Dear Mr Thorne

I am writing concerning content you currently have included on the website
www.27bslash6.com condoning the use of drugs. While I understand that you
may have been trying to be funny, the solicitation of drugs for the intention of
selling or for personal use is a criminal offence under South Australian law.

I advise you to remove the content within 48 hours receipt of this letter.

I can be contacted on (08█████████ or emailed at
m████████████ice.sa.gov.au. I am on duty all day this week from 10am
to 6pm if you have any questions.

Yours sincerely

Michael HARDING
Acting officer in charge
E-Crime Section
SOUTH AUSTRALIAN POLICE

Ph (08) ████████

Government
of South Australia

SA Police
protecting society
from blogs

....

Having written an article where I stated that I wished to purchase drugs
and sell them at a profit, I was contacted by Michael the Police Officer,
who kindly pointed out to me that it is a criminal offense to solicit money
with the intent to purchase drugs and sell them at a profit. As such, I
amended the previous article accordingly.

   Also, I actually spent the weekend in jail recently due to unpaid parking fines. Adelaide police are an interesting bunch, and when I stated
that I was vegetarian, I was given a raw potato to last me the two days.

....

From: David Thorne
Date: Friday 26 February 2010 8:12 p.m.
To: Michael Harding
Subject: Censorship

Dear Michael,

Thank you for your letter. At no time have I condoned the use of drugs.
I simply stated that I wish to purchase and sell them at a profit. I do
however understand the importance of censorship. Without an enforced
system of guidance from agencies such as yours, people would be
forced to exercise their own discretion.

Regards, David

From: Michael Harding
Date: Saturday 27 February 2010 10:27 a.m.
To: David Thorne
Subject: Re: Censorship

David, your obvious disrespect for authority doesn't change the fact that
soliciting money for the purpose of purchasing and selling drugs is a
criminal offense under South Australian law. I advise you to remove the
article and I will check that you have done so by 5pm tomorrow.

Yours sincerely, Michael Harding

From: David Thorne
Date: Saturday 27 February 2010 10:44 a.m.
To: Michael Harding
Subject: Re: Re: Censorship

Dear Michael,

Despite your assumption, I have the highest amount of respect for
authority. I actually wanted to become a police officer but failed the IQ
test when I arrived on time at the correct building.

While not exactly a police officer, when I was about eight I desperately
wanted to be Tom Selleck from Magnum PI. I painted my Standish
Selecta-12 bright red and constructed a mustache by clipping a large
amount of hair from the neighbor's cat and gluing it to my upper lip. This
is how I discovered my allergy to cat hair. As I was dragged to my
neighbor's house, my apology through lips the size of bananas came out
as "Imsryfrctnheroffyrcat iwntdtobemgnumpi." I also wanted to be frozen
and thawed out in the twenty-fifth century due to Wilma Deering's
jumpsuit, but despite emptying the refrigerator and sitting in it for over an
hour, the only result was mild hypothermia and a belting.

I have been considering sitting the police exam again, as protecting
the community from burglars, murderers, and blogs must be very

fulfilling. I am fairly fit due to regularly thinking about jogging, and I once performed a jumping jack. It was unintentional and involved a spider on the bath mat but still counts. I am also experienced in self-defense and recently built a moat. Sometimes, I dress as a French mime and pretend to walk against a strong wind, to the delight of those around me. Everybody loves a mime. This skill would obviously come in quite useful during police stealth operations.

Due to restrictive Australian gun laws, I do not have much experience with weapons, but I did construct my own bazooka when I was about ten using a length of pipe, a securely tightened end cap, a golf ball, and a three-to-one ratio of chlorine and brake fluid. While the design was flawless, the resulting broken collarbone from the kickback, and the two-inch hole through two plaster walls and a television set, brought a swift end to my foray into ballistic research and development.

Regards, David

From: Michael Harding
Date: Saturday 27 February 2010 2:09 p.m.
To: David Thorne
Subject: Re: Re: Re: Censorship

David, this isn't the first time we've received complaints regarding your website. You have until 5pm tomorrow to remove the article, and I'll be checking your website regularly. You might not take this seriously, but I can assure you that we do.

Yours sincerely, Michael Harding

From: David Thorne
Date: Saturday 27 February 2010 3:18 p.m.
To: Michael Harding
Subject: Re: Re: Re: Re: Censorship

Dear Michael,

I do indeed take the matter seriously and will attempt to facilitate your request by 5 p.m. tomorrow despite the fact that I am extremely busy this weekend. I need to bury the two dead backpackers I have in the spare room, as the smell is starting to attract suspicion. And local cats. It is a fairly large job, as one of the backpackers is American and will therefore require a hole several sizes larger than normal. On the plus side, the other is from England, which obviously means no dental records.

I could hire one of those mini bobcat tractors for the day but will probably just let the children out for a game of "Best digger gets food this week." I am sick of hearing them say, "I want my parents" and "Please don't lock me in the spare room again—it smells funny." But many hands, no matter how small, make light work.

Also, I was watching *Crime Stoppers* last night and was wondering if you need anyone to play the perpetrators in crime re-enactments? I have several years' acting experience convincing coworkers that I am listening and care about their relationship issues or what they did on the weekend while really thinking about robots or what would happen if a car made of diamond drove really fast into a wall made of diamond. I would prefer to play either a black professor or an Asian bus driver.

Regards, David

From: Michael Harding
Date: Sunday 28 February 2010 10:26 a.m.
To: David Thorne
Subject: Re: Re: Re: Re: Re: Censorship

I suggest you spend the time deleting the page as you have been requested to do rather than writing about dead backpackers. What is wrong with you?

From: David Thorne
Date: Sunday 28 February 2010 2:02 p.m.
To: Michael Harding
Subject: Re: Re: Re: Re: Re: Re: Censorship

Dear Mike,

My apologies for not getting back to you earlier, I was busy torching my vehicle. Did you know that if you report it stolen, the insurance company gives you money to buy a new one? I usually do this every eleven months, as it saves having to pay for an annual service.

I do not have dead backpackers in the spare room. I was just being silly. There is no space in there due to the hydroponics system, pots, and bags of nutrients. I read somewhere that it is OK to have up to three hundred and seventy marijuana plants for personal use. Correct me if I am wrong.

As I do not have a backyard and the plants take up most of the apartment, I sleep in a hammock stretched between two of the larger trunks. It is like sleeping in a jungle, and sometimes I imagine I am a baby monkey. Due to the twenty-four hour UV lighting, my electricity bill this month is nearly four thousand dollars, but I have an awesome tan.

In regards to the website, rather than deleting the article, I will amend it to be about cats. Is this acceptable to you?

Regards, David

From: Michael Harding
Date: Sunday 28 February 2010 2:31 p.m.
To: David Thorne
Subject: Re: Re: Re: Re: Re: Re: Re: Censorship

It isn't legal to grow even one plant which I'm sure you already know. Possession of less than 100g or one plant has been decriminalized but still carries a fine. Changing the page to be about cats is fine. I will be checking to see if it has been done by 5pm. I strongly suggest that you do so.

From: David Thorne
Date: Sunday 28 February 2010 4:17 p.m.
To: Michael Harding
Subject: Re: Re: Re: Re: Re: Re: Re: Re: Censorship

Dear Mike,

5 p.m. eastern standard time or ours?

Regards, David

From: Michael Harding
Date: Sunday 28 February 2010 4:41 p.m.
To: David Thorne
Subject: Re: Re: Re: Re: Re: Re: Re: Re: Re: Censorship

Ours. I've had enough of your nonsense. If the page is not removed or changed within the next 20 minutes I will be filing an order under the e-crimes act of 2006 to have the website shut down.

From: David Thorne
Date: Sunday 28 February 2010 4:59 p.m.
To: Michael Harding
Subject: Re: Re: Re: Re: Re: Re: Re: Re: Re: Re: Censorship

Done.

Cats
an exciting investment opportunity

As there is no money in graphic design or writing, I have decided on a different career path and am inviting investors to participate in an exciting investment opportunity that promises guaranteed returns in a ready market.

Business Plan

$5,120 in raised capital is required. $5,000 of which is to purchase cats. The extra $120 will go toward purchasing a metal briefcase to put the cats in. Like the ones you see in movies. I have not decided on what kind of cats yet—but whatever young people are doing these days. I will then sell the cats at a profit, and investors will be offered the profits back.

I once drove two hours to buy cats for fifty dollars that turned out to be parsley, which I could have purchased from my local supermarket for around two dollars. This indicates not only a ready and willing market but also a mark-up of 2,400 percent on the initial investment.

I also once paid twenty dollars for cats, which had almost no effect. Many years later, I was told by the person who sold it to me that it was actually a dried-up raisin they had found under the couch and that they'd needed the money for cigarettes.

Return on Investment

Using the formula on the following page of 2,400 percent return, investors can expect a minimum $1,200 return on a $50 initial investment.

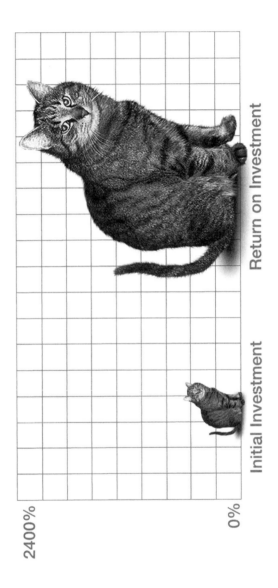

2400%

0%

Initial Investment

Return on Investment

Holly's guide
to the exciting sport
of tennis

Hello, my name is Holly, and I love playing tennis. Not with David, though, because he cheats. Once, while we were watching *Jeopardy,* he forgot to say "What is" before answering the question but gave himself a point, anyway. What is wrong with people? It isn't that hard. Alex gives you the answer and you have to answer with the question. Playing by the rules makes it more fun for everyone. Play it properly or go watch the TV in the bedroom. I don't care if it hasn't got cable; it has the local channels. It's your choice.

Introduction to Tennis

Considered by some a game and by others as the terrifying act of exercising by choice, tennis, invented in 1976, involves fun things to do with racquets and balls. You can swing a racquet. You can hit a ball. Tennis is also an exciting spectator sport that allows people to watch other people swing racquets and hit balls.

Each game lasts for approximately four hours. Three hours of this consists of picking up the balls so that you can hit them again with a racquet. The remaining hour is spent arguing. Variations of tennis include golf, hockey, and Slip 'n' Slide.

Scoring

There are only four basic rules to scoring: If David hits the shot in, then it is out and you get a point. If David hits it out, then you get a point. If at any point David asks what the score is, his inability to pay attention means you get three points. Hitting balls over the fence gives you a few minutes to relax while David collects them, and two points.

A standard scoring sequence consists of "Fifteen love, fifteen all, forty love. I win." It would make more sense to just make it the first to four, but the game was invented by the British, who only discovered consecutive numeric sequencing following the 1982 release of XTC's single "Senses Working Overtime."

If David questions the accuracy of the score, this means he is cheating. Display disappointment at his inability to be trusted and point out that you should be used to his lies because of the time he told you the movie *28 Weeks Later* was a romantic comedy.

Racquet Selection

It does not matter what brand or quality the racquet is, as long as it is pink. It is actually preferable that the racquet is not a recognized brand as this enables you to blame each lost point on it. Reiterate this to David by throwing the racquet in disgust several times per match, and when the racquet fails to return a shot, stare at the racquet with a look of disdain as if to say, "What the fuck, racquet? What are you doing? That wouldn't have happened if you were the kind of racquet Andre Agassi uses." After winning a point, point out the fact that not only was it a point won, but it was a point won with inferior equipment.

Clothing

Before each game, it is imperative to purchase a new outfit. Your top should match the sneakers and shorts should match the socks. If a headband is worn, it should match the racquet, which should match the top, sneakers, shorts, and socks. If David cannot locate his shorts, suggest he wear his yellow swimming trunks with the palm trees and starfish on them because it is just a game of tennis, nobody will be there to see him, and he is not Andre Agassi.

Preparation

Prior to each game, an injury description should be prepared. It does not need to be dependent on the outcome, because "You only won the game because of my possibly broken leg" works just as well as "I won despite my possibly broken leg."

Serving

Every serve David makes is out. Being closer to the area that the ball was meant to be hit toward means your view is the only one that can be trusted and he just thought it was in because he is "looking at it from farther away and on the wrong angle." All serves you make are in for exactly the same reason.

If David mentions that you are not wearing your glasses, state that your vision is clear enough to see through his lies.

Obstruction

Obstruction is an integral component of every tennis match. If David serves a ball that you simply cannot be bothered attempting to reach, calling out "obstruction" means the shot is void and must be made again. It doesn't matter what the obstruction is, a stick nearby or a dog that you saw on the side of the road the previous day while driving to work will do. If David questions the validity of this rule, remind him that it is just a game and that he is not Andre Agassi.

Game Play

A winning shot should be accompanied by a small dance and admonishment if David does not agree the shot was possibly the greatest shot ever made in the history of not only tennis but all sports. A winning shot by David should be met with statements such as "The sun was in my eyes" or "Nobody likes you; you do realize that, don't you?" and a look such as the one you use when you ask him to drive to the shop to get sour cream for the nachos and he comes back with a twelve pack of Bic lighters and a folding chair.

If you are losing the game, it is important that David realizes it is not because he is playing well, it is because you don't care.

Standard procedures include:

1. Hang on—David's serving. I'll put you on hold for a second.
2. Yes, I'm ready. Go ahead and serve.
3. Fuck this—I'm going home to watch *Jeopardy.*

Game, Set, Match

Convention dictates that players shake hands after the match, unless you have lost, in which case giving the finger is acceptable.

If you have won the match, request another. If you have lost, due to the racquet not being the kind Andre Agassi uses and your leg hurting, state that you wish to leave. Do not speak to David on the drive home.

Play the Dixie Chicks CD.

Bob
the rocket scientist

AGL account
there is no such thing
as a portal

Usually when I get a bill, I put it on top of the fridge, figuring that if it isn't red then it isn't interesting enough to be opened. Other times, I grab the mail on my way out and open it while waiting at traffic lights. As was the case with an electricity bill for $766.05. It is not the largest bill I have ever received, but it was enough to make me do one of those double-takes like you see in cartoons and break out in a sweat. My first thought was to move and change my name. When I was about nine, I asked everyone to call me Ace because I liked the band Kiss, but they wouldn't. Later, in my teens, I told someone my name was Renaldo because I thought it was funny, but unlike Ace, it stuck and lasted about two years longer than the five minutes I thought it was funny.

From: David Thorne
Date: Monday 16 August 2010 8:12 p.m.
To: sales@agl.com.au
Subject: Ref. 28941739

Dear Sir/Madam,

I have just received an account for the amount of $766.05. Up until this moment, my accounts have, on average, been around the one hundred and sixty dollar mark, and I doubt the Holtzman field portal experiments I am conducting in my spare room would account for this discrepancy.

Please correct this error immediately by typing in my reference number, clicking on the alarmingly large number, and moving the decimal point to the left. I don't care how many places.

Regards, David

From: Allison Hayes
Date: Tuesday 17 August 2010 9:26 a.m.
To: David Thorne
Subject: Re: Ref. 28941739

Hello David, I have checked your account and the amount of $766.05 correctly corresponds with your usage of 3262 kWh peak and 1982 kWh off peak for the indicated supply period. I dont know what portal experiments are but perhaps it is why you are using more electricity than previously. Please call our toll free number on 1300 133 245 should you have any further inquiries about your account.

Sincerely, Allison Hayes

From: David Thorne
Date: Tuesday 17 August 2010 11:04 a.m.
To: Allison Hayes
Subject: Re: Re: Ref. 28941739

Dear Allison,

Thank you for explaining that the amount correctly corresponds with a number you have based it on. I already called that telephone number and spoke to a robot for several minutes.

While I'm sure you receive a predominantly positive response from those hearing the response "I'm sorry; I didn't get that. Let's try that again" repeated fifty times, I would rather be kicked in the head by a horse the size of ten horses all molded together into one big horse than dial that number ever again. It was incapable of directing me to the correct department despite my responding to each question with the word "exterminate" in a metallic voice.

During school holidays when I was about ten, I attempted to construct a robot from household appliances, which included a blender, an Atari 2600, and a vacuum cleaner. My intention was to have it completed before the holidays ended so that it could accompany me to school and kill Bradley McPherson, who had stolen my Casio calculator watch. After realizing that the project would entail actual engineering knowledge, and being told to "Clean up that fucking mess in the shed," I instead told everyone at school that Bradley's mum had told my mum that he had been born with both a penis and a vagina and had to wear special underpants to keep the two separated.

I also constructed an electric sword around this time after viewing an episode of *Buck Rogers in the 25th Century* where they fought with such. Connecting an electric car antenna to the house mains and holding it with a garden glove, I tested it on my sister's cat. After dissembling the sword to hide all evidence and opening the windows in an attempt to air out the smell of burned hair and cooked flesh, I buried (the appropriately named) Sooty in the backyard. A week later, during a family barbecue, the dog dug her up.

While I cannot go into too much detail regarding my portal experiments—due to the fact that AGL representatives would probably visit me and touch my stuff and say things like, "We are watching you, buddy,"—I have attached a rough diagram that shows that more energy is produced than used, making it unlikely that this is why my account is five times its usual amount.

Regards, David

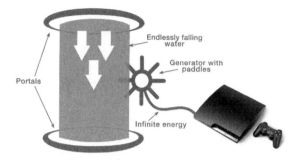

Endlessly falling water

Generator with paddles

Portals

Infinite energy

From: Allison Hayes
Date: Tuesday 17 August 2010 3:19 p.m.
To: David Thorne
Subject: Re: Re: Re: Ref. 28941739

Hello David

The amount of $766.05 is calculated from the meter reading. While I understand your frustration with the automated phone system, we are not able to deal with account inquiries via e-mail and according to my supervisor there is no such thing as a portal so I've no idea why you are sending me pictures of them.

Sincerely, Allison Hayes

From: David Thorne
Date: Tuesday 17 August 2010 4:05 p.m.
To: Allison Hayes
Subject: Snap

Hello Allison,

I am not questioning the calculation; I am questioning the number the calculation is based on. If you accepted cows as payment and I owned two cows, worth forty dollars each, but counted them incorrectly, lost one in a dark forest, and sent you the remaining twenty, would you come out thirty-three dollars and ninety-five cents ahead and call it a perk, or have one cow? Perks are actually one of the only reasons I still bother to turn up for work. While my coworkers are in meetings discussing why the business is going bankrupt, I put office supplies in the boot of my car.

As every meter reading for the last two years at this address has been under two hundred dollars, rather than pay you $766.05, I would prefer to spend that amount on thirty-eight pizzas, ensuring sufficient fat reserves to survive having the heat turned off, or have my apartment lined with polyester socks and wearing a suit made out of carpet—possibly generating enough power to start my own grid company. I would then construct a number, calculate an amount based on this and send out accounts stating that the amount is based on a number and is therefore mathematically correct. If anyone questioned the basis of the number the amount is calculated from, I would simply declare, "I have the power," and point out the scientific implausibility of their experiments, forcing them to investigate other, more viable, designs.

Regards, David

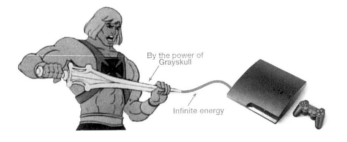

By the power of Grayskull

Infinite energy

From: Allison Hayes
Date: Tuesday 17 August 2010 4:16 p.m.
To: David Thorne
Subject: Re: Snap

Hello David,

Have you bought any new electrical equipment in the last few months that might account for the additional usage?

From: David Thorne
Date: Tuesday 17 August 2010 4:24 p.m.
To: Allison Hayes
Subject: Superconducting quadrupole electromagnets

Hello Allison,

Nothing that springs to mind. I purchased a Large Hadron Collider a few months back, but it has not seen much use. The one time I did manage to get it working, I ended up at the day before I unpacked it, so this wouldn't count.

Regards, David

From: Allison Hayes
Date: Tuesday 17 August 2010 4:31 p.m.
To: David Thorne
Subject: Re: Superconducting quadrupole electromagnets

Whats a hadron collider?

From: David Thorne
Date: Tuesday 17 August 2010 4:38 p.m.
To: Allison Hayes
Subject: Re: Re: Superconducting quadrupole electromagnets

It's kind of like a pressure cooker but with way more dials.

From: Allison Hayes
Date: Wednesday 18 August 2010 11:31 a.m.
To: David Thorne
Subject: Re: Re: Re: Superconducting quadrupole electromagnets

Hello David, I have spoken to my supervisor and if you like I can arrange for someone to come out next week and read the meter again to check if there has been an error.

From: David Thorne
Date: Wednesday 18 August 2010 1:29 p.m.
To: Allison Hayes
Subject: Sanātana Dharma

Hello Allison,

An excellent suggestion. Sometimes the most obvious solution to a problem is the one that evades us most easily. Like a cow in a dark forest.

Regards, David

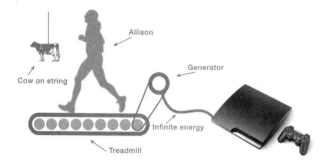

Kaleth
the Adelaide gothic

Hello, my name is Kaleth. My real name is Darryl, but my friends call me Kaleth. I asked them to, and some of them said they would. I am a vampire and a creature of the night, which is why my friend Zothecula and I stand in the middle of the mall during the day discussing bats and being misunderstood.

My cousin Justin wants to be a gothic as well, but you can't just become a gothic, you are either creative and sensitive like I am or you are not. I agreed to meet him at the mall to stand in the middle and discuss bats and be misunderstood, but when he got there it was obvious that his top was actually very dark blue and not black, so I did not let him. Yesterday, while we were standing in the middle of the mall discussing bats and being misunderstood, a group of people called me an Emu. I looked it up on Google, and it turns out that it is a bird that can't fly, so they were wrong, because I can fly. Once, when I was a bat, I flew to my friend Zothecula's house and tapped on his window. The next day he told me that he saw a bat outside his window, and I told him that it was me, but he didn't believe me. Zothecula and I are going to live forever because we are both vampires. We met on an Internet chat site called batsandbeingmisunderstood.com last year, and now we regularly catch the bus to the mall to stand in the middle and discuss bats and being misunderstood together. I met my Internet girlfriend Nightblade on the same site, and we had planned to get married in a graveyard at midnight, but she turned out to be an old guy living in a caravan, so that didn't work out.

I was playing my *Best of Siouxsie and the Banshees* cassette really loud the other day while doing some gothic dancing, and my neighbor slipped a note under my door that read "Turn it down, Batman." He calls me Batman because I painted my front door black with bats on it so that it looks like they are flying out of a cave. One of the bats has my face on it, and my best friend Zothecula said that it is the best painting he has ever seen. If my neighbor knew that I could cast a magic spell that would just kill him straight away, he would be more careful.

Yes, us gothics are more intelligent and sensitive than you, and we do look at things differently, but that doesn't mean that we can't all get along. We understand you, so I think you should at least try to understand us.

Here are some of my paintings. I do them to show others the pain and torment I experience.

The color of my heart.

This is a painting of bats flying around at night. One of them is me.

This one is the inside of a coffin.

This one needs no explanation—it just makes me cry every time I look at it.

Frogs
and temporal distortion fields

....

When I was about ten, my best friend Dominic and I would go down to the creek at the end of our street and play. The creek contained thousands of tadpoles and you could easily find several frogs by lifting rocks.

....

Speaking of my best friend Dominic, he lived just five minutes from my house, with grapevines between the houses. One day he called me to come over and I left right away. As I was walking through the grapevines, I received what felt like a large push from behind and almost fell; when I turned around to confront the person who had pushed me, there was nobody there. I continued to Dominic's house, and he asked where I had been because I had left my house almost four hours earlier. True story. I have, to this day, no knowledge of where the four hours went, but I think I walked through some kind of temporal distortion field, possibly to a far off future where I met my soul mate, we grew old together, and I was then given the choice after she died to return to my own time, the moment I left, with no memory of my future life. This is obviously the most likely explanation.

We would take a frog and insert one of those thin fruit box straws into its anus and blow it up like a balloon. We would then put the frog onto the water and let go and watch it speed across the creek. Sometimes the frogs would burst as we were blowing them up. As the creeks were teeming with the tadpoles, we classed this as no more cruel and unnecessary as throwing the tadpoles at each other from each side of the creek in what we called Tadpole Wars. One day we threw frogs at cars driving past but were chased by a lady, so we didn't do that again. Once, after reading that licking toads would make you high, we dared each other to swallow frogs live. On one occasion my mother opened the freezer to find eighteen frozen frogs, because I had been told that they could be frozen and then revived.

A couple of years ago I was in the area with my son and we went to the creek, but there were no frogs or tadpoles in it. This could be because they have all died out from pollution over the years, but I prefer to think that they are fine and remembered me through some form of inherited group memory and hid. We did find a shopping trolley, though, which entertained my son for about an hour, so that was good.

I thought I would have a lot more to write about frogs, but I am bored already.

Frog Facts

The Brazilian Jungle Frog can mimic human speech and grows to the size of a small child.

Frozen frogs make a healthy and fun addition to any kid's school lunch box.

Mud Frogs can live for up to eighty years but spend all this time in hibernation under dried river mud.

When blended, frogs make an excellent energy drink, which contains 92 percent of recommended daily vitamin intake.

While frogs have a varied diet, which includes nuts and corn, their favorite meal is the cheese quesadilla from Applebee's for $6.69. Due to the fact that frogs do not require oxygen and can withstand extreme pressures, they can often be found searching the ocean floor for their second favorite food, krill. These deep-sea abilities make the frog a perfect companion for skin divers as part of the buddy system. Frogs can also be taught to weld.

Frogs have excellent reception and can be used in place of your standard television aerial.

Frogs are extremely territorial and protect their nests by attending Neighborhood Watch meetings. Frogs prefer contemporary furniture over traditional. A pile of empty flat-pack IKEA boxes at the base of a tree is a sure sign that a frog nest is present.

Placed between tissue paper and under heavy books for a few weeks, a dried frog makes a stunning broach.

There are approximately eighteen thousand varieties of frogs, but most fall into one of three categories: the big frog, the little frog, and the black bear. As the chart below shows, there is a frog in the United States, one in what looks like Japan, and a really big one in Africa.

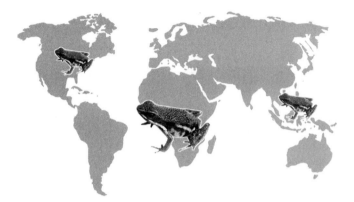

Tom's diary
a week in the life of a creative director

Hello, my name is Thomas, and I run a design agency. You have probably heard of me, as I am known as the Design Guru of Adelaide. Everybody calls me that. You can call me Tommy, though. Or the Design Guru of Adelaide, if you want. Just try it and see how it sounds. No? OK, I wasn't asking you to call me that; I was just saying most people do. It's not a problem—Tommy, then. Or the Design Guru of Adelaide if you say it a few times in your head and find you prefer it because it rolls off the tongue quite well. OK, Thomas, then.

Monday

10:30 a.m.
At work early this morning because I started writing a novel last night and am keen to check if any publishers have e-mailed me with expressions of interest yet. I am about halfway through, and so far it is brilliant. It is about a guy who runs a design agency during the day but at night is a karate soldier with psychic powers. And can fly. And has lots of girlfriends. I am currently looking through photos of me for an appropriate one to use on the cover. One that says "creative genius" but at the same time "Hey." I will probably use the one where I am sitting on a chair, as it will remind people of that statue where the guy is thinking, called Guy Thinking. Or the one of me on the beach, because my hair looks great and I am not wearing a shirt, which will sell books.

12:30 p.m.
Have just ordered a new MacBook Pro because my current one is almost six months old and I cannot be expected to play Solitaire at these speeds.

Staff complained about the speed of theirs when they heard, but I spend four to five hours each day sitting behind them watching what they do and have witnessed, firsthand, Photoshop running fine on the Macintosh IIci they share. I just upgraded it to 8 MB a few years ago and am far too busy to be dealing with their petty issues.

1:30 p.m.

Spent the last hour writing another chapter of my novel. It now spans several millennia, from the nineteenth century to the twentieth, due to the main character being immortal. Having him first jousting redcoats then, later in the novel, time-traveling robots, provides contrast and a break from the parts where he has a lot of girlfriends.

2:30 p.m.

Have been sitting behind the staff having brilliant ideas. I think of things all the time that are brilliant. What is it called when you are a sideways thinker? I am one of those. I usually have about ten sideways ideas per minute. I should probably sit the exam for Mensa. I am just too busy. Just this morning, while shaving my back, I thought how great it would be if my shaver had an MP3 player built in, as I was in the mood for a bit of Seal and that would have made the four-and-a-half-hour process more enjoyable. I would call it the Rave'n'Shave.

3:30 p.m.

Heading out for a drive shortly to buy a kite—they are a great way of meeting new friends. I have a meeting scheduled but have told the secretary that if the client comes in before I get back, to talk about me and say, "I am surprised you managed to get an appointment with him, as he is in high demand and is known as the Design Guru of Adelaide."

4:30 p.m.

Got back in time for client meeting. We agreed on a package that saves me 20 percent on local calls, so it has been a successful day. Heading home because I am exhausted and *Jumper* is on cable.

Tuesday

12:30 p.m.
Just got into the office, as I was up late downloading the iPhone developer's kit. I played a lot of *Space Invaders* on my Commodore 64 when I was young and have a brilliant idea for an app that will make millions of dollars. It is a bit like *Space Invaders* but more like *Frogger.* With a Braille touch screen for the blind.

1:30 p.m.
Spent an hour writing another chapter of my novel. The main character now works as an international fashion model. And has the ability to transport himself to any location on the planet as long as he has been there before.

2:30 p.m.
Since my creative energies are too large to be tethered to one discipline, in addition to becoming a famous author, I have decided to win *Australian Idol* this year. I have my first singing lesson in half an hour. My voice is like one of those mermaids that sings to sailors as they crash onto rocks. But a man version, with a deeper voice, and legs. Although I have the look they are after and perfect pitch and tenor, it makes sense to get a few pointers from a professional beforehand.

3:30 p.m.
Have decided not to win *Australian Idol* this year as I am too busy.

4:00 p.m.
Long day. Heading home after I send out an e-mail to all staff reminding them to refer to me as the Design Guru of Adelaide and describe working with me as "inspiring" when they talk about me with people at the pub or during family dinners.

Wednesday

11:00 a.m.

Late one last night. Decided to go to the pub and stayed for a few drinks even though everyone I knew was leaving when I got there. Guys are uneasy being around me with their girlfriends because they know the ladies are thinking about me naked. Probably lifting·weights or dancing. Luckily, there was a girl at the bar by herself, so I sat down and talked to her about me. Surprisingly, she had not heard of me even though I am very well known and people refer to me as the Design Guru of Adelaide. Unfortunately, she had to leave before she could finish reading the news clippings about me that I keep in my pocket, but she did agree to give me her mobile number, 0123 456789, so will ring her tonight and talk about me then.

1:40 p.m.

Staff member just mentioned that eight years ago I said, "I have full-body cancer with only one year to live, and that's why everybody needs to work quicker." Told them that I never said that and to stop making things up. Anyway, I was talking about another guy who had cancer. He is dead now, so they should show some respect.

2:00 p.m.

Leaving early today to ring the girl I met last night. She will probably want to meet for a drink or come over to my place, so I need to collate the photocopies of news clippings and magazine articles about me into a scrapbook for her and shampoo my chest. I also need to make a mixtape of my favorite songs. I know most of the dance moves to *Disco* by the Pet Shop Boys so will start slow with that before popping and locking for her with some Depeche Mode.

Thursday

9:30 a.m.
Early night last night. Walked into the office talking on phone, telling client I appreciate him for saying I was the most creative and brilliant person in Australia, when the phone rang. Explained to staff that my phone is one of the new iPhones that rings while you are on a call to let you know that someone else is calling and they just haven't heard of it yet. Because their phones are old. And I got cut off at the same time it rang. That's the only reason I stopped talking and looked surprised.

10:30 a.m.
Finishing up the final chapters of my novel. It is now set in a post-apocalyptic future where the polar ice caps have melted, water covers the planet, and people live in floating towns.

11:00 a.m.
I have a meeting to go to in an hour and need to go shopping for something nice to wear, as my green trucker hat does not go with any of my canvas shoes. I should start my own T-shirt company because I have lots of brilliant ideas for T-shirt designs and people would be happy to pay upward of two hundred dollars per shirt if they knew I had designed it. Like Ed Hardy. Except I would have cats on mine because cats are very popular. I would sell them online, and every time someone googled my name it would come up with my T-shirt company and they would buy them. I should also make a website where people can buy my semen. Women would pay thousands for my semen. Because of my creative genes. Like one of those racehorses or a cow with award-winning udders. I would do that if I weren't so busy.

4:30 p.m.
Have just gotten back from a four-hour meeting with a potential client in regard to designing a business card for them. I am very excited about where this could lead, as they are the eighteenth largest supplier of gravel in both the east and east-west suburbs of Adelaide. I will send them a quote in a

few weeks, since they take a long time to write. I could tell they were impressed during the meeting, especially when I explained the need to incorporate cats into the design, as they continually rose, in a manner that can only be described as lengthy standing ovations, then sat down again when I kept talking. One of the female clients was very attracted to me, so I spent an hour showing her color photocopies of my Smart Roadster specs and explained what all the graphs meant. I will send her an e-mail now and tell her my last girlfriend died of cancer or something so that she knows I am available and will attach a photo of me sitting in my car. And one of me wearing jogging shorts so she knows I am athletic.

4:35 p.m.
Heading home, as I am exhausted both physically and mentally after two client meetings in as many months.

Friday

10:30 a.m.
Walked in and had an argument with the secretary. I do not see why I have to justify myself to her. It is my business and therefore my company Visa card. I do not appreciate being questioned. Obviously there has been some kind of mistake and we have been charged $29.95 per month by teenshemale.com in error. It is not her job to ring the bank and question the purchase when I told her I would take care of it even though I am extremely busy.

10:35 a.m.
Have put a password on my computer. Used a random selection of 128 numbers and characters so as to make it impossible for the secretary to guess. Will not write it down anywhere, in case she finds it.

1:30 p.m.
Completed my novel. It is without a doubt the best book ever written and will become a bestseller within weeks. This will mean that I will be very busy

doing promotional tours and replying to people who have written thanking me for sharing my gift, so I will need to tell my staff that I will not be here as often to give them the creative guidance they rely on me for. This will be upsetting, but they have to understand that I owe it to my fans to do book signing tours and appear on *Dancing with the Stars*.

1:35 p.m.

To celebrate the completion of my novel, I invited the staff over to my place to listen to stories about me, but they all had prior plans.

2:00 p.m.

Heading home and calling it a week. It has been a very busy one and therefore productive. Next week is going to be extremely busy as I have decided to write a musical based on my life story. Probably with cats in it as cats are very popular.

Roz
loves Adelaide and owns a plain

Roz Knorr, a pseudonym I will assume unless she is part Klingon, does not like Adelaide. Or perhaps it is just me. She certainly doesn't like my writing and seems to have missed the point that there are plenty of other writers discussing sweatshop children and how man has ravaged Mother Earth. Sometimes it is nice to have a pointless distraction. We can't spend every waking hour kissing trees and throwing paint at women wearing fur coats.

From: Roz Knorr
Date: Monday 12 October 2009 11:56 a.m.
To: David Thorne
Subject: Adelaide loser

Only in a backward town like Adelaide would you get dickheads who would write crap like you. You cant even write well. Thats the result of the sub standard backward schools in Adelaide. Writing about monkeys and children starving. Spend a few nights with the Salvos feeding the homeless so you can write about that and at least people will go to your site and learn something loser. Little dick typical male. Face it when it comes to Adelaide it is full of dumb backward hick arseholes that are totally devoid of social consciousness or culture.

From: David Thorne
Date: Monday 12 October 2009 12:38 p.m.
To: Roz Knorr
Subject: Re: Adelaide loser

Dear Roz,

Thank you for your e-mail. I apologize for the delay in replying. As you mentioned, Adelaide is a tad behind other cities in regard to not only consciousness and culture but also technology. Your e-mail was received by Adelaide's only computer, a 386 housed in the public library powered by a duck on a treadmill, before being relayed to me by Morse code. Should you wish to contact me direct next time, my home number is dot dot dash dot dash dot dot dash.

Regards, David

From: Roz Knorr
Date: Tuesday 13 October 2009 9:18 a.m.
To: David Thorne
Subject: Re: Re: Adelaide loser

Typical coming from such backward piece of crap city like Adelaide. You just proved my point. LOL! Your reply shows what a bacwards hick you and everyone who lives in Adelaide is. I have homes in Hong Kong, Britain, Paris, USA, & Hawai, as well as Australia. I grew up in a house with 11 servants & a chaufer. And honey I have friends living in Laurel Canyon, & California who earn $400,000 a day in rock & roll. Poor Adeliade. No culture and no class. Be careful not to be a victim of a hit & run. Accidents happen all the time, so much cheaper in Adelaide. One phone call . . .

From: David Thorne
Date: Tuesday 13 October 2009 9:51 a.m.
To: Roz Knorr
Subject: Re: Re: Re: Adelaide loser

Dear Roz,

Thank you for your concern and kind offer, but I should be fine for the moment in regard to monetary-based injuries. Recently, I set up a stall at a women's golfing convention with a banner stating "Punch me in the head for one dollar." I made eight hundred and thirty dollars that day. Tax-free. With the money raised, I intend to buy a bigger stall for next year's convention.

It must be nice to own several homes all over the planet. For many years I dreamed of experiencing the culture of Paris, until I realized there would probably be a lot of French people there. They should do something about that. Contrary to your statement regarding Adelaide having no culture, though, there is actually a large and thriving artistic community here, but very little art is produced due mainly to the artists spending all their time displaying their scarves to each other and attending gallery exhibitions for the free alcohol and food, and the chance to wash their armpits in the venue's bathroom.

Regards, David

From: Roz Knorr
Date: Tuesday 13 October 2009 2:14 p.m.
To: David Thorne
Subject: Re: Re: Re: Re: Adelaide loser

You wouldn't know a thing about culture being from Adelaide. You are a bunch of inbred filthy convicts and are all a bunch of no hoppers. I won't even quote you how much money I make from my busenesses that I have in New York, Britain or Japan.

From: David Thorne
Date: Tuesday 13 October 2009 3:02 p.m.
To: Roz Knorr
Subject: Re: Re: Re: Re: Re: Adelaide loser

Dear Roz,

Actually, while Adelaide may commonly be referred to as the "murder capital of Australia" due to having more serial killers per capita than any other city in Australia, it is ironically the only Australian capital city not founded by convicts. Adelaide is also referred to as the "city of churches" due to the fact that there is a church on every corner. It is not surprising therefore that Adelaide also has a long history of child pedophilia. Another common misconception is that due to Adelaide's high number of churches, the city must be a very religious one. In fact, the number of churches is only necessary in order to cope with the number of funerals as a result of the number of murders that take place here.

You are also mistaken in regard to Adelaide containing no hoppers. I myself regularly hop. I am, in fact, the founder of the Adelaide Hopping Club, an organization that meets each Tuesday to hop. We have so many members that it is often standing room only at the meetings. Which is obviously not a problem.

Recently, we have been planning an event in which we intend to hop nonstop from Adelaide to Sydney to raise not only awareness for the sport of hopping but also funds for a new charity we have set up called The Roz Knorr Hopping Foundation, which will provide poor people with no legs a single artificial leg and accompanying hopping instructional video inspiringly titled "Never Give Up Hop."

Regards, David

From: Roz Knorr
Date: Wednesday 14 October 2009 11:16 a.m.
To: David Thorne
Subject: Re: Re: Re: Re: Re: Re: Adelaide loser

You wouldn't know the first thing about charity or giving back to the community. People from Adelaide don't do anything for the underprivileged in society. Go read Naomi Klein's 1999 book "No Logo" and join the ant-globalist movement & start defacing corporate posters in public places with political statements, or visit a sweat shop with 7 year olds in Mexico & blog about it. Until then you are just another selfish parasite taking from this planet. Watch your back. I leave for New York in my private plain this afternoon so I don't have any time for anymore of your pathetic hick town nonsense.

Goodbye David.

From: David Thorne
Date: Thursday 15 October 2009 11:55 a.m.
To: Roz Knorr
Subject: Re: Re: Re: Re: Re: Re: Re: Adelaide loser

Dear Roz,

Thank you for excellent suggestions. Unfortunately I cannot afford the airfare to Mexico and even if I did, I do not know any seven-year-olds to take. It's a pity, as I have heard that you can get really cheap soccer balls there. Coincidentally, I too have a private plain. It is actually more of a field but, going by the number of backpackers discovered buried in the area, quite private regardless. I was sitting in the middle of it reading your correspondence regarding poorly written books and eighties political statements when I realized you raise a valid point. I organized a garage sale in which I sold my neighbor's outdoor furniture and used the proceeds to move to Nimbin. I spent today rubbing my body with crystals, dancing to Fleetwood Mac, writing poetry about rain drops, and braiding my leg hair to form rope, which I have used to construct dream catchers to sell at the local commune shop. As the commune rejects the concept of money and accepts only happy thoughts in exchange for goods, I am writing this using my laptop powered by karma as an alternative energy source. This e-mail is being sent with an attachment of love.

Regards, David

From: Roz Knorr
Date: Friday 16 October 2009 10:41 a.m.
To: David Thorne
Subject: Re: Re: Re: Re: Re: Re: Re: Re: Adelaide loser

Dangerous ground loser. You do not know who you are dealing with. I know a lot of people.

From: David Thorne
Date: Friday 16 October 2009 11:09 a.m.
To: Roz Knorr
Subject: Re: Re: Re: Re: Re: Re: Re: Re: Re: Adelaide loser

Dear Roz,

Yes, I realize you must know many people. I calculate the six real estate agents, pilot and co-pilot of your private plain, your rock and roll friends making $400,000 a day, plus the eleven servants and chauffeur makes a total of twenty-two. I am assuming the chauffeur is the person you intend to have me run over by, if not, then twenty-three. This total does not, of course, include the people you know from the Salvation Army, anti-globalist movements, sweatshop owners, the shop assistant at your local XXL Golf Pants'R'Us, or members of the K.D. Lang Fan Club.

Regards, David

From: Roz Knorr
Date: Friday 16 October 2009 2:01 p.m.
To: David Thorne
Subject: Re: Re: Re: Re: Re: Re: Re: Re: Re: Re: Adelaide loser

E-mail me agian and you will be sorry. Bye.

From: David Thorne
Date: Friday 16 October 2009 2:07 p.m.
To: Roz Knorr
Subject: Re: Re: Re: Re: Re: Re: Re: Re: Re: Re: Re: Adelaide loser

■■■ ● ● ●   ■■ ● ■■ ■■   ●

Hello, my name is Craig,
and I love dolphins

I love dolphins so much. They are so graceful, sleek, acrobatic, and wet. If I were a dolphin I would be one of those brave ones that fights sharks. I wish I were a dolphin. If I were a dolphin, I would swim alongside boats and jump out of the water to the awe of spectators, and they would feed me fish. That would be heaps easier than catching them.

I read somewhere that the dolphin in *Flipper* was actually several dolphins, since the dolphins kept dying. Or it might have been Skippy the kangaroo—I forget which. Either way it is very sad. Once when I was swimming, I found myself caught in a rip and was carried far out to sea. After several weeks of treading water, I became too weak and gave up hope. As I slipped from the surface and slowly sank like that guy in the movie *Titanic,* I was rescued by a friendly dolphin, who carried me back to his family and fed and nursed me back to health before constructing a small raft out of kelp for me on which I sailed back to shore. Ever since that day, I have devoted my life to collecting the most beautiful dolphin sculptures in the world.

Here are just a few of my favorites:

The most beautiful and magical creatures of the sea, these magnificent dolphins are captured in their wondrous movement atop the crystal waves. As if mirroring the ocean, the waves sparkle with prismatic colors and dazzling lights. I have this on the dashboard of my 4WD; people often remark on its unique beauty. At almost sixty centimeters height it does obstruct some view but is semi-transparent, so I do not feel it causes any problem.

The only way you sleep through this alarm is if you do it on porpoise. Every morning I wake up to the pleasant sound of dolphin laughs, it makes me chipper, ready for the day, and aroused.

In this deliciously decorative delight, a dolphin frolics merrily amongst lacy turquoise reefs. With a charmingly crafted shell for keepsakes, this pleasing sculpture is a dolphin lover's dream! I keep this on my desk at work and use the hanging basket to put my mobile phone in. My ringtone is a dolphin call, so every time my phone rings it is like the dolphin is singing to me. I call this dolphin Carl.

Seashell, dolphin, and coral reef night light. Simply beautiful. If I were a dolphin I would definitely live in an underwater paradise such as this. Leith and I would be the dolphins on the right and the other dolphin would be a friend dropping by. They would remark on what a beautiful home we had, and then we would eat that fish.

One of my favorites: Three marbleized dolphins form a cozy nest, awaiting the pleasant aromas, which will soon drift from the urn of this absolutely stunning oil warmer. Sometimes I light a candle, add my favorite oil, and sit watching it while listening to dolphin calls on my iPod.

A mother dolphin teaches her baby the ways of the sea on this blue-glass carved art piece with tea light holder. If I were the mother dolphin, I would teach my baby dolphin that life has no set path but that which you choose.

Dolphin Facts

Dolphins taste like chicken. Really good chicken.

Dolphins can hold their breath for up to eight weeks but need to surface occasionally to look around, as they cannot open their eyes under water.

Singing to a dolphin will make it love you and be your friend for life.

Have you ever noticed
the beauty of a baby's smile?

Hello, my name is Barry. I am available and looking for that special woman. She has to enjoy never leaving the house, cleaning me with a damp cloth, and experiencing the beauty of a baby's smile. I placed an ad in the singles' columns that simply read: "Woman wanted." I felt it would be superficial to include that she must be athletic and named Candy. I will screen them when they call.

I read recently that the earth is not actually a sphere and is compressed at the poles and bulges at the equator, where the world spins the fastest. This means that objects at the equator are under less gravitational pull and therefore weigh less. I have calculated that I would lose almost six hundred kilograms by moving my bed ten meters closer to the equatorial line. This is a lot of effort for little outcome, but I did change position by eight centimeters today. Changing positions once a week allows mum to wipe sections of my body according to a rotation schedule. It also burns calories and is part of my regular exercise routine. In the future, there will be televisions that change channels when you blink your eyes.

My Life Story
I was born in a small village near a secret government-testing complex. As part of an experiment in human/pig cloning, I led a happy childhood, often seen rolling through the streets of the village. Sometimes I would also take my scooter. When I grew to manhood, I was placed inside a magnetically shielded device designed to compress my molecular structure into a sin-

gularity point using my body's own gravitational fields. Now that I am a singularity point, I have the ability to see through all time and space.

"The View from My Bed," By Barry

I have two buckets, green and blue.
On Tuesdays a nurse comes and cleans my poo.

My Favorite Bible story

Once when baby Jesus was in the desert, he turned some snakes into a small hut, where he lodged for the night.

Sell me your car
for cheap, as it is not a very good one

I quite liked my vehicle and was not overly happy about selling it. To ensure a quick sale, I advertised it for $5,200—around half its market value. Recently, I saw a used Bose Acoustimass subwoofer and speaker system, which retails for well over a grand, advertised for $200 ono. I contacted the seller, writing, "Excellent price; I will take it." I actually paid $250 because he threw in speaker stands and I had budgeted twice that amount for a system half as good. I did not offer him $75 for it or haggle, because selling an item at a low price, for whatever reason you have, is trying enough without squirrels like Brian offering peanuts for it.

From: Brian Lawrence
Date: Wednesday 26 May 2010 11:04 a.m.
To: David Thorne
Subject: Car

Hi I saw your ad for the car I checked redbook and its not worth much because its pretty old and they hve lots of problems with the waterpumb and stuff. can come and have a test drive now if your home. will you take $1800 cash for it?

From: David Thorne
Date: Wednesday 26 May 2010 11:46 a.m.
To: Brian Lawrence
Subject: Re: Car

Dear Brian,

Thank you for your enticing offer. I was moments away from swapping the vehicle for three magic beans, so your timing is impeccable.

When I was about ten, I swapped my Standish Selecta 12 racing bike for a broken microwave oven. Planning to construct a mind control ray, I connected the innards of the dismantled microwave unit to a tape recorder (which repeated the words "Let David paint his bedroom walls black") and plugged it into the mains. Unfortunately, the only results were being thrown across the room, receiving third-degree burns to my hands and arms, and forgetting how to do long division.

Disheartened that there have been only eighteen inquiries for the vehicle, despite it being advertised over an hour ago, I am not only prepared to deliberate your offer but willing to throw in a pair of pants (beige, size 32L) and a four-kilo bag of squirrel food to sweeten the deal.

Regards, David

From: Brian Lawrence
Date: Wednesday 26 May 2010 3.17 p.m.
To: David Thorne
Subject: Re: Re: Car

ok. does the car take petrol or diesel? I can come now if your home. whats the address? what the fuck would I want squirel food or pants for?

From: David Thorne
Date: Wednesday 26 May 2010 4:08 p.m.
To: Brian Lawrence
Subject: Re: Re: Re: Car

Dear Brian,

They are quite nice pants. Squirrel food enables you to entice squirrels into your garden. I often sit on my back deck watching them run back and forth excitedly like Ricky Lee at an all-you-can-eat buffet. I wish I were a squirrel. Sometimes I talk to them and promise that if they speak to me I will not tell anyone else that they can do so. They haven't yet. I doubt I would be able to keep their secret, anyway, so it is probably for the best. I have named one Brian. Being an ugly squirrel, he was constantly ridiculed by the others until I tied a shiny ribbon around his neck. Now, as he passes, the squirrels point and declare, "Look at that squirrel! He must be rich or a secret agent."

In regard to fuel type, the vehicle runs on a special blend of 9,000-octane rocket fuel and plutonium. The tachometer reads 179,300 but has clocked several times due to the vehicle being capable of covering distances in excess of twenty thousand kilometers per second. The advantage of this is that due to relativity I always arrive several minutes before I leave. Often, if I am very late for work, I simply drive around the block a few times and arrive before anyone else. Once, when I misjudged the accelerator pedal for the brake while entering the car park, I arrived at work the previous day and helped myself finish a project. We then went for a beer together, but having nothing much to say, we went our separate ways, promising to catch up sometime but probably won't. If truth be told, he was kind of annoying and smoked all my cigarettes.

The address is Top of the Forest (High Ground), 100 Aker Wood East. It has a green door. You can't miss it.

Regards, David

From: Brian Lawrence
Date: Wednesday 26 May 2010 7:24 p.m.
To: David Thorne
Subject: Re: Re: Re: Re: Car

I dont give a fuck about stupid squirels. i hate squirels. is that a street address what suburb? do you want to sell the car or not? I can come and look now and the car looks white in the photo is it white or silver? do you have a cd player?

From: David Thorne
Date: Thursday 27 May 2010 10:06 a.m.
To: Brian Lawrence
Subject: Re: Re: Re: Re: Re: Car

Dear Brian,

The vehicle employs the same paint technology as the stealth bomber. Sometimes it appears to be white and other times as small shrubbery. This has proven quite handy during police chases, especially in garden centers. The interior boasts a myriad of colors, thanks to hand-quilted Mennonite seat covers, while the ceiling features an eighteen-by-twelve-meter medieval tapestry of some guy in armor stabbing a fat peasant for offering threepence for his horse.

I do have a CD player; thanks for asking. And although the vehicle does not, it does feature a Rank Arena record player in the boot. As long as you do not exceed ten kilometers per hour and avoid speed bumps, the sound reproduction far surpasses that of compact disc technology. Along with the pants (beige, size 32L) and four-kilo bag of squirrel food, I will throw in the *Christmas with Boney M* LP and *Forever & Ever* by Demis Roussos, which includes the hit single "My Friend the Wind."

Regards, David

From: Brian Lawrence
Date: Thursday 27 May 2010 1:34 p.m.
To: David Thorne
Subject: Re: Re: Re: Re: Re: Re: Car

you can keep the squirel food and pants what have squirrels go to do with the car?I can get a black BMW for how much you want for your car. why are wasting my time? are you fucking stupid?

From: David Thorne
Date: Thursday 27 May 2010 1:51 p.m.
To: Brian Lawrence
Subject: Re: Re: Re: Re: Re: Re: Re: Car

Dear Brian,

I do apologize. I assumed from your initial offer that wasting each other's time was the premise of our relationship. The vehicle has been sold, at the asking price, but the pants (beige, size 32L) and four-kilo bag of squirrel food are still available if you want them.

When I was young, I had an Auntie named Phyllis who owned a glue gun and believed homemade presents were far superior to store-bought ones—despite her artistic level being just below that of a blind quadriplegic monkey. I once received, inside a large box with a shiny ribbon, a Christmas tree snowman ornament consisting of a foam ball with plastic hat, sequins for buttons, and face drawn on with a Bic pen. For my birthday. In February. Her presents were quietly referred to as "shit in a shiny ribbon."

I'm sure you will be much happier in your BMW. As you drive down the street, people will probably point and declare, "Look at that guy! He must be rich or a secret agent."

Regards, David

From: Brian Lawrence
Date: Thursday 27 May 2010 5:21 p.m.
To: David Thorne
Subject: Re: Re: Re: Re: Re: Re: Re: Re: Car

go fuck a squirel

Simon's guide
to wilderness survival

Hello, my name is Simon, and I have been lost thirty-six times, which makes me an expert. Once when I was lost in the desert, I survived by absorbing the moisture from the air through my skin like a frog and feeding on krill. Another time when I was lost in the Antarctic, I fashioned a snowmobile from ice, and rode to safety. I have compiled this complete guide to wilderness survival to ensure you too can survive, should you find yourself lost, in almost any environment.

Survival Tip #1

If you have water with you, drink it all immediately. There is a good chance you will be rescued before long, so it is pointless being dehydrated. If you do run out of water, the trick to finding more in the wilderness is to remember that water always flows downhill. Find a hill and wait at the bottom. I read somewhere that if there is no water available, you can drink your own urine, so I always take a two-liter bottle of it wherever I go just in case.

Survival Tip #2

Do not eat the bright purple mushrooms. Once while lost, I found and ate some bright purple mushrooms, figuring such a friendly color could not possibly be dangerous. A short time later, a beetle and I discussed the differences between the director's cut of *Blade Runner* and the cinematic release. Always remember that bark is an excellent source of nutrition and can be prepared simply by marinating overnight and cooking for twenty minutes in a preheated oven at 240 degrees Celsius.

Things that should not be eaten:

Bright purple mushrooms
Rocks
Cha-Chi's Mexican Restaurant food
Wasps

Survival Tip #3

Building yourself a shelter is an integral part of survival. A small bungalow or cottage will be sufficient unless you have a lot of furniture. Always remember that when tiling a roof, it is important to use a rope and harness to avoid falling. If you do fall, land horizontally with your arms and legs stretched out to maximize surface area. Always check with your local council on required permits prior to building. Protect yourself from hungry animals by fortifying your shelter. A wall of no less than two meters with a lockable gate should be sufficient. Always build your wall out of noncombustible materials, as wild animals will often attempt to gain access by using fire. Befriend large animals such as bears to protect you from smaller ones. A bear can easily be mollified if you run toward it yelling.

Materials that are not suitable for building shelter with:

Water
Angry words
Live ants

Survival Tip #4

Building a fire without the use of matches or a lighter is a simple matter. Most forest fires are caused by lightning strikes, so run a steel cable from the top of a tall tree to a pile of sticks, and then be patient. Construct your fire under a group of trees and stack large piles of leaves around the edge to serve as wind-breaks. Wolves are attracted to firelight but have a highly developed sense of smell and detest the odor of petrol, so be sure to douse the surrounding area and yourself well.

If you do not have petrol with you and wolves enter your campsite, curling up into a small ball and making a high pitched sound like a wounded bird will confuse and deter them. If you are being attacked by a wolf, do not accidently grab a snake to fight it off with. If you have emergency flares, taping several dozen to your legs and setting them off at the same time will allow you to hover above the wolves for several seconds, safe from their snapping jaws.

Survival Tip #5

Having the appropriate clothing and medical equipment in preparation for any weather condition or emergency situation is the key to survival. If you are camping in a cool climate such as the Antarctic, make sure you take a scarf. Watching the movie *Castaway* will give you an idea of what items would be useful should you find yourself lost for several years, and comes down to personal preference. If I were Tom Hanks, I would have taken several hundred cartons of cigarettes and a suitcase of pornography.

I read somewhere about a guy who, while camping, cut his leg, and as he was sleeping, a spider laid eggs in the wound. I would rather amputate my leg than have baby spiders hatching in it, so a surgical-grade bone saw is an essential component in any backpack. It is always better to preempt these things, so any limbs that receive cuts, scratches, or bites should be removed immediately.

Survival Tip #6

Find some means of alerting rescuers to your whereabouts. If you are lost in a desert, writing a large SOS in the sand with your water is an effective means of drawing attention. If you are lost in a jungle, a simple two-way radio can be constructed from kits available at any Tandy or RadioShack store. Waving your arms at passing rescue planes expends precious energy, so it is better to dig a small hole, lay in it, cover yourself with leaves to keep warm and relax while you wait for them to find you.

Use the time you are waiting to be rescued wisely. Sort your DVD collection into alphabetical order or fix that broken tap that you have been meaning to for months but did not get around to because it would mean driving to the hardware store and buying a new rubber washer. Scrapbooking is, apparently, a fun and satisfying hobby.

Having someone to talk to will help the time pass much more quickly. The last time I was lost and feeling lonely, I constructed company to talk to from mud. I called her Anne, and after realizing we had a lot in common, we fell in love. Sadly, she disappeared a few nights later during a rainstorm, and though I searched desperately for her throughout the wilderness for many weeks, I eventually gave up hope and sought respite from the outside world inside a dam, where I lived for eight years with my pain and a family of angry beavers.

Survival Tip #7

If you become bored while waiting to be rescued and decide to walk, it is helpful to have a map. As you have no way of knowing where you may become lost, a map of everywhere is required. Simply marking everywhere on the map you are not will pinpoint where you are. A simple compass can be constructed by rubbing a small round pebble up and down polyester slacks to generate static magneticity, then floating the pebble in a small pool of water. The pebble will sometimes face north.

Keeping a collection of pebbles in your pocket is also handy for when you come to a stream, as you can use them as stepping-stones. In case of deeper rivers, it is wise to carry a collection of larger rocks in your backpack at all times. If the river is still too deep, constructing a canoe can easily be accomplished by pouring a mixture of liquid polymer and setting agents into a precast mold.

Professional
photography tips
with Thomas

Hello, my name is Thomas, and I am a professional photographer because I bought a digital camera.

Tip 1 • *How to become a professional photographer*
Buy a digital camera.

Tip 2 • *Tricks of the trade*
Have a look on the camera; somewhere, probably on the top or back or somewhere on the front or sides, there will be a button or dial marked "A." This does not stand for "Automatic," as some amateurs think, but "Awesome." Leave it on this all the time.

Tip 3 • *Photography courses*
There is no need for even a basic photography course, because once you buy a digital camera you will be a professional photographer like me. Not as good as me, though.

Tip 4 • *Lighting*
You will need some light; otherwise the photos will come out a bit too dark. Usually you can fix them in Photoshop, but some light to begin with is good.

Tip 5 • *Subject matter*

Yes, it does. Don't take photos of girls leaving the high school from your car, as the fine is $360 and a year's probation.

Sunset from my rooftop.

View of city from my rooftop.

The plant on my rooftop.

Some people that once came to visit me on my rooftop. Or my toes—I am unsure.

Ten jobs
I would rather have than mine

I get up after hitting the snooze button a minimum of six times. I make a coffee, then sit in the shower drinking it and smoking cigarettes until the initial agony of knowing I have to spend another day with my coworkers dissipates. I generally spend this time trying to calculate the pros and cons of just not turning up. I know they will bitch, but their opinions mean little to anyone, so sometimes I just stay in the shower for an hour and then go back to bed. If I do decide to go in, I sit in an office the size of a wardrobe and temperature of a kiln prostituting myself by spending the day making poor products look appealing so that people will be tricked into buying them. This pretty much sums up the entire design industry. Sometimes I grumble and whine out loud so that people think I am working, but I am on the Internet instead. It has lots of things on there I like. As I am possibly the laziest person I know, the design industry is the only field I can survive in. I would last less than an hour doing manual labor of any form, and I often cope on less than two hours' sleep a night, so anything requiring alertness or intelligence is out of the question. As is anything requiring personal hygiene. This leaves either taxi driving or my boss's position. As his job role consists only of pretending to talk on the phone, passing blame, and downloading pornography, I am more than qualified.

#1 Fortune Cookie Writer

As far as writing jobs go, this would probably be the easiest, as the pages are very small. When I was at school, I had an English teacher named Judith Bowman who would make us read a novel every few weeks and write a two-page essay on each. This would not usually be an issue, as I enjoy reading, but Mrs. Bowman loved Agatha Christie novels so would force us to read only these. As my interest in reading about French inspectors on trains is on equal par with being molested by a drunk uncle, I handed in my two-page essay on two pieces of paper measuring two-by-three centimeters each (arguing that the size of the two pages had not been indicated at any time) with the words "Reading the novel *Murder on the Orient Express* is" on one piece, and "less enjoyable than being molested by a drunk uncle" on the other. This did not go down as well as might have been expected, and I was forced to rewrite the essay, which this time I began with "Being forced to read Mrs. Bowman's own personal preferences in literature is less enjoyable than being molested by a drunk uncle, which is why I chose to read *Ender's Game* by Orson Scott Card instead . . ." If I were a professional fortune cookie writer, among the standard messages of promised hope and riches, I would include statements such as "I am sending you this message from the future. Robots will take over in four days; leave the city immediately" and "Judith Bowman has anal warts."

#2 Park Ranger

Sometimes when I am at work and have had enough of moving pixels around the screen, I will grab my keys, saying, "I have to go to a client meeting. I will be back in an hour," and run out the door before anybody can question who the meeting is with. Then I go shopping for cleaning products or to a movie. If I were a park ranger I would tell everyone that I had a meeting with a sick bear or something, then go for a canoe ride.

#3 Drug Dealer

It would seem to me that being paid to provide something that makes people happy would be one of the most satisfying professions available. A while back, my mother visited a Tasmanian region where they grow opium poppies for medicinal purposes and brought me back a seed she had "found." I planted it in my front yard and several weeks later it bloomed. Having read L. Ron Hubbard's *Mission Earth* series, which included detailed instructions on processing opium, I used a scalpel to cut lines in the black center, then dried the milky substance, resulting in about half a tea-spoon of white powder. That night, my friend Kas came over to my place with his entire CD collection to listen to, and we decided to try some of the powder. A short time later, with the live version of Gary Numan's "Down in the Park" playing on loop, we were both standing completely naked in the bathroom shaving our entire bodies, following a discussion about how nice it would be to have smooth skin like an eel. I do not recall much of the rest of the evening, but I awoke to find myself wearing a pillowcase with holes cut out for my arms and head as a shirt and Kas asleep on the sofa wear-ing the same, plus 3D glasses. Before waking and leaving later that after-noon, Kas swapped me his entire CD collection for the remainder of the powder.

#4 Wind Turbine Technician (specializing in aerotechatrons)

Everyone loves wind turbines because they are so big and white and sym-bolize clean, renewable energy and environmental responsibility. I knew a girl once who had a poster of one on her wall, and when I asked if she was an environmentalist, she answered, "No, I just like them," which is fair enough. Everyone does. I have never heard anyone say, "God, I hate wind turbines," so if my business card said Wind Turbine Technician rather than Designer, I would probably receive the pity look a lot less. The only problem is that I would have to pretend to care about the environment. There is an old saying that "This is not our planet. We are just looking after it for our children," but in thirty years when my offspring complains that we trashed the planet, I will say, "That's what you get for all the crap Father's Day pres-ents." Once, while talking to a girl at a bar, I lied to her about my job, telling her I was a wind turbine technician (specializing in aerotechatrons), be-cause I was bored and thought it would be funny. After a few beers, I put my arm out to lean against the bar and my hand slipped, sending my neck into the corner of the bar and leaving me unable to breathe for a few min-utes. After assuring her that I did not require medical assistance, she stated that she had to go and asked for my business card. Forgetting my deception, I handed one over, and while she stood there reading the card, frowning, I asked her out, but she said no.

#5 New Zealand Tourism Operator
This would give me plenty of spare time, as nobody wants to go there.

#6 Adult Movie Star
Being paid to do something pleasurable would be nice, so it is strange that prostitution or starring in pornographic movies is seen as a demeaning profession. While attending uni, studying the artistic equivalent of prostitution (graphic design), a female friend and I decided to make a "home video" and borrowed a large video camera with tripod from the university media department for the night. Foregoing script, we were in mid performance when my leg developed a severe cramp, and I kicked the tripod, causing the camera to topple forward and crash into the back of my head, cutting a two-inch gash. I was kept at the hospital overnight after receiving fourteen stitches and arrived home the next day to find the camera had been returned to the media department, complete with video cassette still in it. A week later, I received a letter from the media department lecturer stating that the media equipment is available only for school projects, not "C-grade pornography."

#7 Accident Claim Investigator
Having a job where people tell you a story and you say, "I don't think so," seems like it would be a lot of fun. I have been in a total of three vehicle accidents. The first occurred when I was driving on a dirt road in the rain, lost control, and hit a cow. The second occurred while driving home from my friend Simon's place. While at his house for a coffee, I attached a rubber spider on a string to the inside of his cupboard with sticky tape so that the next time he opened it to grab a coffee mug, the spider swung out at him. The reaction was more than expected: Simon screamed, threw himself

backward onto the floor, and actually cried. Later that afternoon as I was driving home, I lowered the sun visor and the rubber spider, which Simon had placed there in what he felt was appropriate retaliation, fell forward onto my lap. I pressed hard on the brake and turned the steering wheel, sending the vehicle into a spin and clipping a white Mercedes before ending up in an elderly man's front hedge. The third occurred many years ago while driving to uni one morning. A girl driving a Ford Laser pulled up at the traffic lights next to me, and I noticed she was wiping tears and looking quite angry. As there is nothing as attractive as an angry and upset female, I came up with an ingenious plan: The next time she stopped at lights, I would "accidently" tap the back of her car, then get out, talk, exchange numbers, and get married. As she was pulling to a stop, I edged forward, but she braked more suddenly than I had expected, and I slammed into the back of her car hard enough to see her head flap around like a rag doll. After pulling over, exchanging details, and offering to drive her to the hospital for the cut on her forehead, I asked her out, but she said no. On all three occasions, I was assigned an accident claim investigator.

#8 Parking Inspector

Although there would obviously be many benefits to being a parking inspector, the knowledge that every day I would be making the world a better place would be the most satisfying aspect. They would try to pay me, and I would put my hand up and say, "No, the important contribution I make to society is payment enough."

#9 Forest Fire Lookout

As far as I can tell, the position consists entirely of sitting in a very tall cubby house, looking out the window. As you would be able to see for miles around and tell if anyone was coming, you could do anything you wanted in between reporting over the radio that you have not seen any forest fires yet. I would probably watch a lot of pornography and do drugs. When I was about ten, a friend of mine and I built a cubby house in the tallest tree in our backyard using wooden planks stolen from the neighbor's fence. Late one evening, while my parents were at a marriage counseling session, I was in the cubby house (as it overlooked the neighbor's bedroom), when a strong breeze caused the cubby house to collapse, pinning me between the floor and a fallen wall. Unable to call out or move due to the crushing weight, I remained there the entire night, falling asleep at one point but waking when it started to rain, before finally being rescued the next day when the neighbor let his cat out and heard my soft cries for help. While I was at the hospital, the neighbor took back his planks.

#10 Doctor
Because nurses are easy.

Professor Thomas
explains the mysteries
of science

Hello, my name is Professor Thomas. People ask me many scientific questions, and I know all the answers because I have the Discovery Channel at home. Perhaps you would like to come over and watch it with me. I have a rooftop as well.

Perpetual Motion

Is perpetual motion like when you fall down a bottomless pit?
Kind of, but it's more like when you put two ice cubes next to each other and they never melt because they just keep each other cold forever.

What if you put two ice cubes next to each other and dropped them down a bottomless pit?
They would drift apart and melt, unless you glued them, but then they wouldn't really be touching.

Leap Years

I like having an extra day. Why can't we have them every year?
There is a good reason you have them only once every four years. It's like chocolate. If you have it too often, you get too used to it, then you need to eat more. Then we've got too many years and everyone lives too long. This would have serious consequences on the circle of life.

Stars

There are stars born every day. People who believe in the science of stars are called Scientologists.

Tides

Sometimes the ocean water is high, but sometimes it's low because the moon is magnetic and it attracts the water.

I thought magnets only attracted metal.
Water's a type of metal. It is also one of the noble gases.

The Water Cycle

Water dies, then decomposers break it down into organic matter. Then it rains water seeds, and when the water seeds mix up with the decomposed water, lakes grow.

Hydrogen As a Fuel Source

Can we use alternative fuel for petrol in our cars?
Only certain cars.

Which cars?
Hydrogen is two-thirds water; so, cars that are one-third water.

Really?
Yes, because humans are 80 percent water, so we use hydrogen and not gasoline, and most cars are around 5 percent; but if the car is 20 percent or more water, then it can run on hydrogen.

Like boats?
Yes, exactly like boats.

Absolute Zero

Absolute zero is when it can't get any colder. It could get infinitely colder, but it wouldn't be any more cold.

Relativity

Einstein's theory of relativity is very complicated and can be almost impossible to understand, but $E=MC^2$ means when you go really fast, time goes slower because you get there earlier.

Black Holes

Space is like a bathtub, and you fill it with light, and black holes are where the light drains out.

Where does the light go?
It goes back into space as light-vapor, and when it condensates, that's how a sun is formed.

So then suns are really clouds of light?
Yes, and then they rain sunshine.

25 minutes on Chatroulette
is like a drill to the head

The problem with Chatroulette.com and other video-based communication is the fact that people can see you. As it takes me at least four hours just to do my hair, this is simply not practical. I generally write in tracksuit pants and a T-shirt while eating pizza, which would be unfair to the other parties to have to view. Having heard a lot about Chatroulette, I decided to have a look. For every ten video connections, eight of them were fat people playing with their penises. Apart from a couple of interesting people I met, it was possibly the most pointless website I have ever been on.

Partner

You

☐ Auto start ☑ Clean chatlog ☐ Chat sounds

>*Connected*

hi

Hello. Star Wars fan?

no

What's the deal with the Chewbacca costume then?

> *Your partner disconnected. Reconnecting...*

Partner

You

☐ Auto start ☑ Clean chatlog ☐ Chat sounds

>*Connected*

Cool shirt. Linux fan?

thanks dude

Do you think penguin would taste more like fish or chicken? Or a combination of both? They are a type of chicken but eat a lot of fish so I think the latter.

wtf? a penguin isnt a chicken

It's like a chicken. They both can't fly and are more agile in the water than on land. If I was a penguin I would steal fish from the other penguins as I have seen documentaries where penguins get flipped in the air by killer whales so there is no way I would go swimming. It just wouldn't be worth the risk. I would probably just eat other penguins as I read somewhere that they taste like a cross between chicken and fish.

> *Your partner disconnected. Reconnecting...*

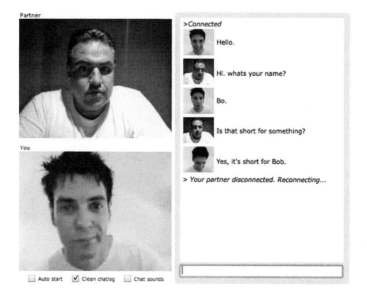

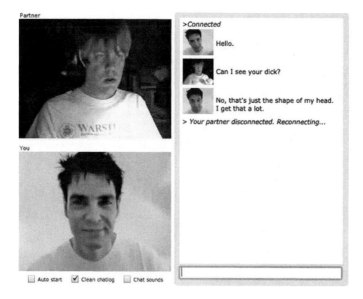

Partner

You

☐ Auto start ☑ Clean chatlog ☐ Chat sounds

>*Connected*

 Hello my name is mike i am in germany i am a student and am 24 old. How are you today and where are you today what country are you in. are you well?

 Whoa there Charles Dickens. I didn't sign on here to proof read a novel.

> *Your partner disconnected. Reconnecting...*

Partner

You

☐ Auto start ☑ Clean chatlog ☐ Chat sounds

>*Connected*

hello how ar you?

About time. I have been waiting for over twenty minutes. This is possibly the worst online support I have ever experienced. I purchased a stereo from you guys two weeks ago and the remote control did not come with batteries. Is this an omission or am I expected to purchase my own? I have the new Miley Cyrus CD and was looking forward to boot-scooting. Did you know that she is Billy Ray Cyrus's daughter? That is simply way too much talent to be in one family. What's your favourite Billy Ray Cyrus song?

> *Your partner disconnected. Reconnecting...*

Tom's haircut
rumors proven unfounded

Rumors that Thomas takes a photo of Carol Brady to the hairdresser have been proven unfounded. Here is finally conclusive evidence that there are indeed considerable differences between the two haircuts. Tom's hair is a shade darker and Carol's has slightly more body—possibly due to the two using different shampoo and conditioning products—Carol uses Johnson & Johnson brand, while Thomas uses the natural oils from his body, which Lillian harvests for him using a custom-made spatula.

Note:

This page does not take into account the dimensional differences between Carol's head and Tom's head.

Photographic Evidence 1
Shows Tom's hair does not have highlights toward the sides.

Photographic Evidence 2
Shows Carol Brady's hair has a lighter hue with highlights toward the sides.

Mattel® Wednesday
using the Magic 8-Ball to answer e-mails

....

I sent an e-mail to a friend recently, asking several different questions, and he replied with the single answer, "Yes, probably." It was obvious that he had either not bothered reading the e-mail or could not be bothered answering my questions. The next day I replied to e-mails by using a Mattel® Magic 8-Ball™ to generate random answers.

....

From: Simon
Date: Wednesday 4 Feb 2009 9:38 a.m.
To: David Thorne
Subject: No Subject

Have you got a typeface called Garamond Semibold? I have the Garamond and bold and italic but not the semibold. I am doing a poster for Cathy and I reckon garamond would look good.

From: David Thorne
Date: Wednesday 4 Feb 2009 10:02 a.m.
To: Simon
Subject: Re: No Subject

As I see it, yes.

From: Simon
Date: Wednesday 4 Feb 2009 10:43 a.m.
To: David Thorne
Subject: Garamond

Which one? Yes you have the typeface or that it would look good on a poster?

From: David Thorne
Date: Wednesday 4 Feb 2009 10:52 a.m.
To: Simon
Subject: Re: Garamond

Concentrate and ask again.

From: Simon
Date: Wednesday 4 Feb 2009 11:14 a.m.
To: David Thorne
Subject: Re: Re: Garamond

What the fuck? I need the typeface Garamond. Have you got it or not?

From: David Thorne
Date: Wednesday 4 Feb 2009 11:18 a.m.
To: Simon
Subject: Re: Re: Re: Garamond

You may rely on it.

From: Simon
Date: Wednesday 4 Feb 2009 11:29 a.m.
To: David Thorne
Subject: Re: Re: Re: Re: Garamond

Send me the typeface dickhead.

....

From: Mark Pierce
Date: Wednesday 4 Feb 2009 2:08 p.m.
To: David Thorne
Subject: Hey

Hey. Are you at work?

From: David Thorne
Date: Wednesday 4 Feb 2009 2:25 p.m.
To: Mark Pierce
Subject: Re: Hey

Signs point to yes.

From: Mark Pierce
Date: Wednesday 4 Feb 2009 2:53 p.m.
To: David Thorne
Subject: Re: Re: Hey

What? Can you drop over on your way home from work and help me lift a piece of glass up onto a table? It is too heavy to lift.

From: David Thorne
Date: Wednesday 4 Feb 2009 3:22 p.m.
To: Mark Pierce
Subject: Re: Re: Re: Hey

My sources say no.

From: Mark Pierce
Date: Wednesday 4 Feb 2009 3:49 p.m.
To: David Thorne
Subject: Re: Re: Re: Re: Hey

Are you serious? I tried lifting it a bit at a time and sliding books under it but I need heaps more books. Can you come for a quick drive now?

From: David Thorne
Date: Wednesday 4 Feb 2009 4:02 p.m.
To: Mark Pierce
Subject: Re: Re: Re: Re: Re: Hey

Ask again later.

From: Mark Pierce
Date: Wednesday 4 Feb 2009 4:57 p.m.
To: David Thorne
Subject: ?

Are you going to help me on the way back from work or not?

From: David Thorne
Date: Wednesday 4 Feb 2009 5:16 p.m.
To: Mark Pierce
Subject: Re: ?

It is decidedly so.

From: Mark Pierce
Date: Wednesday 4 Feb 2009 5:24 p.m.
To: David Thorne
Subject: Re: Re: ?

Good. Fuck you are annoying sometimes.

....

From: Justine Murphy
Date: Wednesday 4 Feb 2009 8:14 p.m.
To: David Thorne
Subject: Tree frogs ppt

Hi David, you forgot to send the attachment on your last e-mail. Can you send it again please?

Justine

From: David Thorne
Date: Wednesday 4 Feb 2009 8:51 p.m.
To: Justine Murphy
Subject: Re: Tree frogs ppt

You may rely on it.

From: Justine Murphy
Date: Wednesday 4 Feb 2009 9:15 p.m.
To: David Thorne
Subject: Re: Re: Tree frogs ppt

Ok. Can you resend it to me then please?

From: David Thorne
Date: Wednesday 4 Feb 2009 9:26 p.m.
To: Justine Murphy
Subject: Re: Re: Re: Tree frogs ppt

Without a doubt.

From: Justine Murphy
Date: Wednesday 4 Feb 2009 9:44 p.m.
To: David Thorne
Subject: Re: Re: Re: Re: Tree frogs ppt

???? Did you attach it?

From: David Thorne
Date: Wednesday 4 Feb 2009 9:51 p.m.
To: Justine Murphy
Subject: Re: Re: Re: Re: Re: Tree frogs ppt

Don't count on it.

From: Justine Murphy
Date: Wednesday 4 Feb 2009 10:27 p.m.
To: David Thorne
Subject: ?

Are you fucking with me? Just attachment it ass hat.

....

From: Simon
Date: Wednesday 4 Feb 2009 11:28 p.m.
To: David Thorne
Subject: No Subject

Are you online?

From: David Thorne
Date: Wednesday 4 Feb 2009 11:37 p.m.
To: Simon
Subject: Re: No Subject

Concentrate and ask again.

From: Simon
Date: Wednesday 4 Feb 2009 11:41 p.m.
To: David Thorne
Subject: Re: Re: No Subject

Fuck you.

CCTV
a busy day in the
design studio

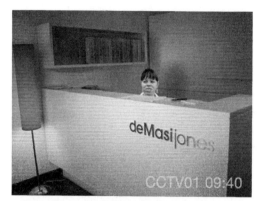

9:40 a.m.
Shannon arrives and
looks out window.

11:58 a.m.
Shannon gets
petty cash.

12:01 p.m.
Shannon "pops out to get lunch and do some things."

1:50 p.m.
Shannon looks out window.

3:47 p.m.
Shannon looks out window.

4:11 p.m.
Thomas leaves for
meeting with himself.

4:12 p.m.
Shannon diverts
phone upstairs
because she has to
leave to "do some
stuff."

Highlights of South Australia, Part 1:
The Monarto Zoo

How is it that Victoria and Queensland can even hope to compete for tourism dollars when South Australia is home to THE Montarto Zoo, featuring a theoretical plethora of wild beasts? Sitting on an ex–school bus with fifty other people as you drive through gates is exactly like being on an actual savanna in South Africa.

Monarto Zoo is always coming up with new advertising to get people to visit. The problem is that when people do visit, they come back and tell people that there are no animals there. If I were the manager of Monarto Zoo, I would have photographic, life-size cardboard cutouts of animals placed throughout the park and drive the bus too fast for people to notice they are not real. Once word got out that Monarto "does actually have animals" and people started visiting, we could afford to replace the cardboard animals with animatronic animals.

My offspring and I went to Monarto Zoo, thinking we could drive around the park as you see people in the movies do, having a monkey try to pull off one of our side mirrors or lions lying on the hood of our car.

We boarded a thirty-year-old school bus, then waited forty minutes for it to fill with people. We were especially lucky to be sitting opposite a mum with a baby that had bright yellow feces leaking out from its diaper. The bus traveled for about ten minutes before stopping to open gates. This happened about twenty times before we saw what was possibly a giraffe lying down. It was too far away to tell whether it was alive, and a few children started asking if it was OK, so the bus drove on.

The gate system is worth mentioning, as it consists of driving up to a gate and pressing a button, the gate rolls open over the space of several minutes and the bus drives through to the next gate and waits for the previous gate to close before opening the gate in front. As this happens at least seventy times, it should be added as a key highlight in promotional brochures. After another several gates, we saw a shed that apparently had a rhino in it, which was quite exciting. We then entered several gates and saw some goats. After an hour and several more gates, we returned to the center where we could buy stuffed animals made in China.

When his grandma asked him what the best part had been, my offspring replied, "The drive home," which I thought was pretty funny, but he wasn't joking.

Highlights of South Australia, Part 2:
St. Kilda Swamp

Only forty minutes' drive from the city is one of Adelaide's most enticing tourist attractions. For a reasonable admission fee of around twenty dollars, families can walk through a swamp along a looping boardwalk. Not all the way, of course, because the boardwalk is broken in places, but the high likelihood of the boardwalk collapsing at any moment only adds to the excitement.

On arrival at the St. Kilda mangroves, you make your way through the Interpretive Center, where they have mud and insects displayed so that you can see them before you enter the swamp. Unfortunately, the day we went, the Interpretive Center was closed, probably due to the staff having a meeting about mud and insects. A sign informed us that they were sorry about not being there but we could enter the swamp via a side gate after leaving money in an honor tin. Though my son attempted to access the contents, it was firmly padlocked.

Checkpoint 1

Passing several signs warning us of snakes, we reached the boardwalk and entered the swamp. After pretending to push each other off the boardwalk into the mud for several minutes, we reached the first checkpoint. Checkpoints consist of slightly wider sections of the boardwalk, with signs explaining that the swamp contains mud and insects. There are twenty checkpoints.

Checkpoints 2 to 8

The mud is worth mentioning, as there were hardly any insects the day we visited. It is very deep in parts and not in others and has millions of spiky roots sticking out of it like semi-submerged hedgehogs. According to the brochure, the mud is teeming with life, but we did not see any. Interestingly enough, the brochure also mentioned that dolphins enter the swamp in search of food, but as they would require one of those ride-on boats with a big fan on the back like the dad drove in the television series *Gentle Ben,* this is quite unlikely. The people who wrote the brochure covered themselves, though; each statement regarding the wide and exciting range of animals to be seen began with "Depending on weather conditions . . . ," so they could have added tigers, polar bears, and elk to the list without any risk of litigation. We did see a dead cat, but that was not listed in the brochure.

Checkpoints 9 to 13

While traversing the next few checkpoints, we played a game called "What we could be doing instead?"

Checkpoint 14

Despite the noticeable lack of other visitors to the swamp, as we progressed to checkpoint fourteen, a father and two children approached us along the boardwalk from the opposite direction, and we gave each other sympathetic and understanding nods as we passed.

Checkpoints 15 to 19

We progressed through checkpoints fifteen to nineteen fairly quickly, driven on by the fact that I had left my cigarettes in the car. With only one checkpoint to go and the car in view, we came to a dead end, where the boardwalk had collapsed. Despite seriously considering jumping the five-meter gap, braving the millions of spiky roots sticking out of the mud, we were forced to turn back and retrace our journey.

Seb & Holly pause from using their mobile phones and games consoles to pose for a photo in one of the more picturesque regions. The natural beauty reflected in the wonder on their faces.

Checkpoints 19 to 1

On the way back we pretended to push each other off the boardwalk into the mud, and since Seb was annoying me, I pushed him off the boardwalk into the mud. Due to his new sneakers being cased in twelve inches of solid black mud, he did not speak to me for the rest of the walk back, which was nice.

Shannon asks a favor
after denying me
petty cash

From: Shannon Walkley
Date: Monday 07 June 2010 12:14 p.m.
To: David Thorne
Subject: Help

I just got a message about static ip and I cant login to my hotmail?!?

From: David Thorne
Date: Monday 07 June 2010 12:26 p.m.
To: Shannon Walkley
Subject: Re: Help

That message refers to static electricity. Turn off the computer, remove your shoes so that there is good contact between you and the floor, and keep both hands firmly on the keyboard for about ten minutes before turning your computer back on. This will discharge any residual static IP. Try to remain as still as possible during the process, as movement, especially while wearing synthetic clothing, will generate more. Are you wearing polyester pants today?

From: Shannon Walkley
Date: Monday 07 June 2010 12:32 p.m.
To: David Thorne
Subject: Re: Re: Help

Im wearing jeans.

From: David Thorne
Date: Monday 07 June 2010 12:38 p.m.
To: Shannon Walkley
Subject: Re: Re: Re: Help

Then you should be fine. You may need to repeat the process two or three times to ensure full static IP discharge.

From: Shannon Walkley
Date: Monday 07 June 2010 12:46 p.m.
To: David Thorne
Subject: Re: Re: Re: Re: Help

ok thanks.

Hello, my name is Lucius,
and I am a straight man

I hope this page lets us get to know each other, and maybe we can watch football together and other stuff that friends do. But just normal stuff, because I am not a gay man.

Star sign
Taurus the lion king.

Favorite color
All of them. Every color on our planet is beautiful.

Height
While most females describe me as small, my height is an attribute, as I am able to hide in small spaces. And everybody loves hobbits. *Lord of the Rings* was a great movie; it was written by Peter Jackson, who also makes cigarettes.

Special skills
I am probably the best at Photoshop in the world. If there were a Jedi ranking for Photoshop skills, I would be a Jedi Master. Wiggling my mouse with the same dance-like grace of a lightsaber in the hands of a Grand Master Jedi. Like Yoda. But not as tall.

Hobbies

Collecting and swapping unicorn figurines on eBay. I love unicorns. I think it is very sad that we allowed them to become extinct. Man is a selfish animal sometimes. We could have shared the world with them, but we hunted them for the magical powers their horns possessed.

If I had a unicorn I would meet it in the forest and be gentle with it until the day it trusted me enough to let me ride on its back. Once when I was out dancing, I met some guys who were going to get tattoos, so I joined them and got a unicorn on my chest. It has a rainbow-colored horn, which I was told symbolizes intelligence and beauty, so that is appropriate for me.

Me and my best friend Aaron. Aaron has great tattoos. I was going to get a tattoo but wasn't sure which of my designs was the best. They were all so great. Besides, having a tattoo might spoil my chances of getting signed to an international modeling career or something like that.

Aaron giving my skin a close check for discoloration after being out in the sun. He is very sun-safety conscious and always makes sure we "slip slop slap" before going out. He's a great friend and very caring. Nothing gay, though, because we are both straight.

The atmosphere during Mardi Gras was amazing. The sounds and smells and colorful floats. I wanted to drive one, but they wouldn't let me. I would have been a heap's better driver than the guy driving it. I could go heaps faster. I met lots of new friends and had a really good time. Nothing gay, though, because I am straight and they all knew that.

Love letters from Dick,
Rove's biggest fan

....

I wrote a stupid post a while back about the television host Rove and his dead girlfriend. Basically asking why no one mentions his dead girlfriend. I also stated that I thought she got off easy: "Not tonight, dear. I have cancer." Of all the messages I received proclaiming me to be a prick for making statements about his dead girlfriend, Dick's were the most entertaining for me because he just kept going. Unfortunately, I have not received any correspondence from Dick for a while. I will assume he has been arrested by the beard police. This is saddening, since it seemed as though no matter what nonsense I sent him, he would reply in anger.

....

From: Richard Matthews
Date: Tuesday 6 May 2008 7:42 p.m.
To: David Thorne
Subject: Rove

Fuck you retard wydont you shut up! he dident ask for his gilrfriend to die so use your brain to work out how you would feel and just fucken shutup!

From: David Thorne
Date: Tuesday 6 Nov 2007 8:04 p.m.
To: Richard Matthews
Subject: Re: Rove

Dear Dick,

Thank you for your recommendation. I am currently writing a television script that I think you would be perfect for. It features a genius of superior wit and intellect who uses his uncanny abilities to protect the innocent. Aided by his loyal pet, masturbating monkey, he endeavors to right wrongs and solve crimes. At the end of each episode he will leave us with a profound, thought provoking, and politically correct statement such as "Don't leave your pet in the car with the windows up" or "Fuck you, retard—wydont you shut up?"

An important part of the character development, as I see it, would be the developing relationship between yourself and the masturbating monkey. The show will be titled *Monkey Dick* (a combination of private dick and the pet monkey, similar to *Canine Cop*), and I do hope you will make yourself available for this opportunity.

Regards, David

From: Richard Matthews
Date: Tuesday 6 May 2008 8:17 p.m.
To: David Thorne
Subject: Re: Re: Rove

Fuck you coksucker you should be ashamed of what you wrote that was wrong ad you know it How wud you feel if you were rove?

why dont you fuck off.

From: David Thorne
Date: Tuesday 6 May 2008 8:42 p.m.
To: Richard Matthews
Subject: Re: Re: Re: Rove

Dear Dick,

You're correct. My statements were uncalled for and unquantifiable in any manner. I apologize without reserve and ask for nothing but your understanding. I hope, in time, you can come to forgive me for such contemptible statements. If I could retract my statements I would, but I do not have a time machine.

I wish that I did have a time machine. I would take my MacBook Pro back to 1984 and visit Steve Jobs. After selling my laptop to him for millions I would return to the present. I could do this several times, as each time the present technologies would have changed. It is a flawless plan, I am sure you will agree, lacking only the availability of time/dimension manipulation technologies.

Regards, David

From: Richard Matthews
Date: Tuesday 6 May 2008 9:02 p.m.
To: David Thorne
Subject: Re: Re: Re: Re: Rove

That didnt even make any sense. why dont you stop wasting your time and get a girlfriend!

From: David Thorne
Date: Tuesday 6 May 200 9:06 p.m.
To: Richard Matthews
Subject: Re: Re: Re: Re: Re: Rove

Thank you for the excellent suggestion, Dick. I contacted your wife and we are now seeing each other.

From: Richard Matthews
Date: Tuesday 6 May 2008 9:17 p.m.
To: David Thorne
Subject: fuck off

youve obviously got no firends!

From: David Thorne
Date: Tuesday 6 May 2008 9:28 p.m.
To: Richard Matthews
Subject: Re: fuck off

You got me, Dick. You are correct; I have no friends. I am lonely and sad. I am currently sitting in a cave by myself, sustaining myself on beetles, powering my laptop by an ingenious array of pulleys and flywheels constructed from small lizards and tree sap from the local flora. I came here to escape my family, friends, industry associates, acquaintances, and the lady next door who was spying on me, in the hope of completing my novel titled *Why are there so many dickheads messaging me?* I have made the dedication out to you, Dick, and will endeavor to send you a copy once it goes to print.

Regards, David

From: Richard Matthews
Date: Wednesday 7 May 2008 10:37 a.m.
To: David Thorne
Subject: Re: Re: fuck off

Your a moron muthufuka!!!!

From: David Thorne
Date: Wednesday 7 May 2008 11:52 a.m.
To: Richard Matthews
Subject: Re: Re: Re: fuck off

Well done, Dick. That sentence included a word containing more than three syllables—I am assuming "muthufuka" to be one word in your dimension. As I mentioned, I am currently writing a novel and would be honored if you would concede to being the editor. I realize that you must be in great demand, with a long list of literary achievements, and I am less than worthy of your mastery in this area, but an opportunity such as this could simply not be passed by. I will attach the manuscript and look forward to your positive response.

Regards, David

From: Richard Matthews
Date: Wednesday 7 May 2008 2:18 p.m.
To: David Thorne
Subject: Re: Re: Re: Re: fuck off

youve got mental problems wanker and dont call me dick. your the dickhead!

From: David Thorne
Date: Wednesday 7 May 2008 2:44 p.m.
To: Richard Matthews
Subject: Re: Re: Re: Re: Re: fuck off

Dear Dr. Dick,

Thank you for that in-depth psychoanalysis that is so accurate as to be uncanny. As your professional diagnosis has clearly outlined, I do, indeed, have mental problems. It is a degenerative disease that causes a small part of my brain to die every time I receive a message from the kind of person that collects *Star Trek* DVDs and listens to Jimmy Barnes (yes, I read your profile). Little more can be done except to write a letter to your university, in particular your psychology and psychiatry lecturers, congratulating them on producing such an amazing pool of talent.

Regards, David

From: Richard Matthews
Date: Wednesday 7 May 2008 2:52 p.m.
To: David Thorne
Subject: Re: Re: Re: Re: Re: Re: fuck off

fuck you whats wrong with Star Trek? your a wanker

From: David Thorne
Date: Wednesday 7 May 2008 3:19 p.m.
To: Richard Matthews
Subject: Re: Re: Re: Re: Re: Re: Re: fuck off

Nothing is wrong with *Star Trek,* Dick. I enjoy science theory myself, and some of the episodes were not completely embarrassing. I was tempted to write something derogatory and perhaps even draw attention to the fact that the only time in any of your e-mails you have used correct spelling, grammar, punctuation, or capitalization is when you wrote the name *Star Trek,* but I was fearful that your army of Klingon warriors might attack and shoot colorful laser rays at me, causing me to have to land on a planet inhabited by aliens who speak English and look exactly like humans apart from ripples on their noses while I perform plasma warp drive repairs.

Regards, David

From: Richard Matthews
Date: Thursday 8 May 2008 9:27 a.m.
To: David Thorne
Subject: your a wanker

You must be fat and sad and ugly!

From: David Thorne
Date: Thursday 8 May 2008 4:11 p.m.
To: Richard Matthews
Subject: Re: your a wanker

Thank you, Dick. I am touched by your concern for my health, happiness, and social acceptance. I actually am not fat and would usually be described as a bit too skinny. I have been contemplating reverse liposuction, a technique where they basically transfer liquefied body fat from one patient to another.

Having looked on your profile and seen your photo, I was hoping we could help each other out here—I figure some of the fat from just one of your cheeks could help add many kilograms to my current body weight. I realize this would leave you a tad lopsided, so if we take the fat from your other cheek we could sell it to the Japanese. This commercial venture would effectively pay for the initial operation and save several whales in the process. I think you will have to agree this is a socially responsible course of action.

In regard to being sad, aren't we all from time to time? As I am sitting writing this on my laptop in bed while my girlfriend watches *Family Guy* on the 52-inch plasma screen in her underwear, I can't help but think how much happier I would be if she was Brooke Satchwell, was wearing latex, and we were in Bora Bora; so I guess, happiness being relative and on a comparative scale, you are correct.

As for being ugly, I am actually extremely attractive, with god-like features and the body of a Calvin Klein underwear model, due to being born with what is termed the "drop-dead gorgeous" gene, but I can't help feeling life would be much easier if I were, indeed, ugly. How's it working out for you?

Regards, David

From: Richard Matthews
Date: Thursday 8 May 2008 4:21 p.m.
To: David Thorne
Subject: Re: Re: your a wanker

You think you are fucking clever. Im a primary teacher and the kids in my class write better than you moron! kiss my arse.

From: David Thorne
Date: Thursday 8 May 2008 4:29 p.m.
To: Richard Matthews
Subject: Re: Re: Re: your a wanker

Now I am actually horrified. My son is in primary school, and I had the assumption that the adults I leave him in the care of would generally have a higher level of education than his. Just out of interest, can I ask if you have ever had sex with one of your students?

From: Richard Matthews
Date: Thursday 8 May 2008 4:37 p.m.
To: David Thorne
Subject: Re: Re: Re: Re: your a wanker

I teach 3rd grade deadshit

From: David Thorne
Date: Thursday 8 May 2008 4:46 p.m.
To: Richard Matthews
Subject: Re: Re: Re: Re: Re: your a wanker

My question still stands.

From: Richard Matthews
Date: Thursday 8 May 2008 4:58 p.m.
To: David Thorne
Subject: Re: Re: Re: Re: Re: Re: your a wanker

Suck my cock fuckhead

From: David Thorne
Date: Friday 9 May 2008 6:03 p.m.
To: Richard Matthews
Subject: Re: Re: Re: Re: Re: Re: Re: your a wanker

Thank you, Dick. I will take your offer of oral sex as a peace offering but
will have to decline. While I appreciate the gesture, I am very much
straight. I am flattered and even a little curious but feel it would be better
if we refrained from giving in to desire at this stage in our relationship,
and besides, I would not want to risk doing anything that may damage
our friendship—which I have come to value very much.

From: Richard Matthews
Date: Friday 9 May 2008 11:18 p.m.
To: David Thorne
Subject: Re: Re: Re: Re: Re: Re: Re: Re: your a wanker

what? your an idiot im not gonna compete with an idiot anymore. burn in hell wanker not writing any more to you!

From: David Thorne
Date: Saturday 10 May 2008 1:07 p.m.
To: Richard Matthews
Subject: Re: Re: Re: Re: Re: Re: Re: Re: Re: your a wanker

Compete? I wouldn't attempt such a foolhardy exercise. I am possibly the least competitive person I know and am, in fact, the current national loser in the Who is Least Competitive Championships, where trying to win will make you lose. Trying to lose makes you win, which makes you lose. Not trying at all makes you lose, which makes you win, which makes you lose.

From: Richard Matthews
Date: Saturday 10 May 2008 4:40 p.m.
To: David Thorne
Subject: Fucken loser

Yeah your right you do lose. That was the biggest heap of shit i have eva readwhat was that even suposed to mean? dont emai me back your an idiot.

From: David Thorne
Date: Sunday 11 May 2008 11:13 a.m.
To: Richard Matthews
Subject: I want to touch your beard

I am very hurt by your comments, Dick, and I am not quite sure how to take them. Are you saying it is over? With time and a series of expensive counseling sessions, I may see my way through it. If you would be interested in, perhaps, attending some of these sessions together, I believe we may resolve our differences. It's the little things, isn't it, Dick? The little things that you found cute in the beginning of our relationship have become the catalyst for this anger. I can change for you, Dick. I love you.

From: Richard Matthews
Date: Monday 12 May 2008 10:28 a.m.
To: David Thorne
Subject: faggot!

you are a fucken idiot!!! I dont have time to read you stupid shit. What are you even wriing to me for ? I think you are doing it just to annoy me fuckhead

From: David Thorne
Date: Monday 12 May 2008 10:51 a.m.
To: Richard Matthews
Subject: Re: faggot!

I confess. You have caught me out, Dick. Alternative motives may have included "using dick as entertainment," "playing with dick," or even "let's get dick heated," but yes, your supersleuth detective skills have once again outwitted me and centered in on the fundamental reason.

Please find attached a check made out to you for a copy of your book, *Detective Dick's Deduction Dictionary*. I would also like to sign up to receive your monthly newsletter, and please book me in for your course "Deducing Dick." If I use my credit card to purchase the full two half-hour lessons, will I receive the Sherlock Holmes–style cap and curved wooden pipe at no added cost? I have my own magnifying glass. Sometimes I use it on ants. Not to cook them, just to warm them on cold days or get a little fire going for them.

Regards, David

From: Richard Matthews
Date: Monday 12 May 2008 11:09 a.m.
To: David Thorne
Subject: Re: Re: faggot!

Stop messaging me

From: David Thorne
Date: Monday 12 May 2008 11:22 a.m.
To: Richard Matthews
Subject: Re: Re: Re: faggot!

OK.

Life-size Lucius™
free cutout doll

A while back, I indicated in a certain article that the purchase of a certain T-shirt comes with a free Life-size Lucius™ doll. Due to having completely made this up, the doll was not delivered with the product, so I have provided this page for those who feel hard done by.

Sexy time Lucius. Not just sexy underparts, sexy underparts full of luciusness. Like a boy scout, Lucius is always prepared and knows the best way to bait a trap is with love.

Hell's Angel Lucius. He's a bad boy, ladies, playing by his own rules and showing an utter lack of respect for authority apart from the police, road rules and signs.

Shower time Lucius. Scrubbing up and shaving down for a big night out. He's fresh, fragrant and economical due to a single bar of soap lasting several years.

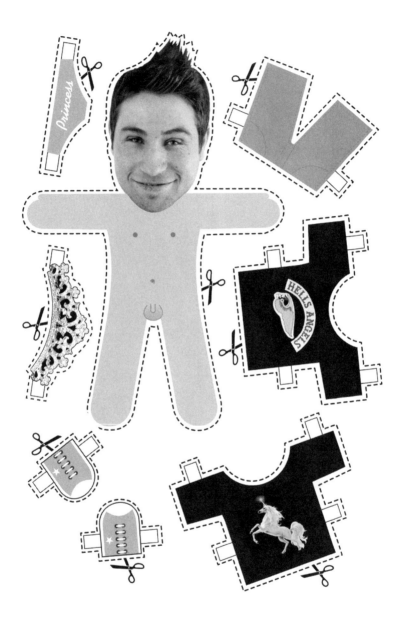

Guns, baseball caps, and pickup trucks:
3 weeks in the USA

Flying out from Sydney Airport

Sydney Airport incorporates an astonishingly clever luggage trolley system called Smarte Carte. Basically, you pay four dollars and load up the trolley, then enter the terminal. At this stage you have to go up an escalator that does not fit trolleys. Luckily, after removing your luggage and journeying to the top of the escalator, there is another set of trolleys you can pay four dollars to use. You can then use the trolley for a few minutes until you reach the international terminal transfer train that does not allow trolleys onboard. Once the train reaches the international terminal, you pay four dollars for a trolley, which will enable you to take your luggage around a corner, where there is an escalator that does not fit trolleys but has more trolleys at the top for four dollars so that you can transport your luggage around two corners before reaching another escalator that does not fit trolleys. Having exhausted both your budget and patience, you carry your bags the rest of the way. Luckily, the crowds part for you, due partly to you dripping in sweat, but mainly due to your "I will stab you" expression, so that you can arrive at the check-in counter and pay two hundred thirty dollars in excess baggage weight fees.

United Airlines

Many years ago, during a traditional family Christmas gathering, the family dog, named Gus, gained access to and consumed a one-kilogram tub of butter that had been left out of the refrigerator. He then proceeded to vomit up the entire kilo under the table (along with his prior meal of dog food and pieces of Christmas turkey). The similarity, minus a thin piece of three-day-old tomato and cold spinach, to the gelatin egg porridge I was served onboard the fourteen-hour United Airlines flight from Sydney to San Francisco was disturbing. I also suspect Gus's version may have contained more nutritional value. Luckily, my meal included a plastic cup of water, so using the power of imagination and a plastic spork, I pretended it was a thin soup and made it last for over an hour.

Although hungry and bored, I was lucky enough to have an overweight American girl sitting in front of me with her seat reclined, thus allowing close inspection of her dandruff. As her hair was very dark, by blurring my eyes I was able to pretend I was looking out of the window at a star-filled night and, at one point, made out the Big Dipper.

Waffle House

Famished after spending a total of thirty-six hours on flying buses and waiting in flying bus stations, salvation presented itself in the form of what is, without question, America's finest restaurant chain. If I were a food critic being asked to write about the meal and experience at Waffle House, my review would contain just two words, one being an expletive and the other "Yes." Possibly accompanied by a pencil sketch of two fat people giving each other a high five. The only negative aspect of the meal was that our waitress, Shauna, hung around and kept going on about her dying child and the cost of cancer medicine in the hope of a large tip, but seeing through this ploy, we snuck out without paying and stole a Waffle House coffee mug in the process.

Snow

I had never seen snow before visiting the U.S., and while those around me complained about their vehicles sliding off the road and not being able to get out the front door, I secretly hoped the snowfall would reach several feet and trap me there for months. My first snowball throw ever was a head shot, and taking into account the excellent degree of distance and trajectory analysis, I would have thought my girlfriend, Holly, would be impressed rather than driving off. Faced with the prospect of spending the night outdoors many miles from civilization, I built a snowman to ward off wolves while I started work on an igloo. After two hours of work resulting in a pile of snow with a hollowed out cave large enough only for my head, I had to hide my relief when Holly came back, proclaiming to her that I would have been fine due to having read the novel *My Side of the Mountain* and that I was not crying—it was just a bug or dust or something in my eye.

Walmart

The first time I went to Walmart, I showered, shaved, dressed nicely, and did my hair to the bemusement of those with me. The second time, I went unwashed, in my pajamas, at 3 a.m. to buy a gun. In Australia, we have a nationwide ban on anything even remotely gun-shaped. When I was about ten years old, there was an elderly man, living across the road, named Mr. Anderson, that I (innocently) drove insane through a sequence of events over twelve months, which included painting his windows black, believing he would wake up and think it was still nighttime; tying his lawnmower to the back of his car so he drove off with it; and putting several packets of raspberry Jell-O crystals in his fish pond. The day I dipped tennis balls in paint and threw them at his house obviously broke him, and he came out screaming and waving a rifle before being arrested. I did not see Mr. Anderson after that, but I am sure everything turned out fine and that he looks back on those times with fond memories.

Guns

Having purchased a heavy gauge shotgun and armor piercing rounds from Walmart for the equivalent price of a carton of cigarettes in Australia, I befriended a local farm boy named Chuck by making up Aboriginal words and telling lies about Australian fauna (it is now a fact in Virginia that koalas, known as Boogawigs in the native Aboriginal language, communicate with each other through song and weave themselves jackets from gum leaves during winter). Chuck drove us in his red pickup to George Washington Forest to drink beer and kill something. Four drink bottles and a cinder block lost their lives that afternoon before a deer walked into the clearing and was shot in the leg. As the humane thing to do is never leave an animal wounded, and having run out of ammunition, we clubbed it to death with the butt of our rifles, which took about an hour, then tied it to the hood of the pickup truck and drove home listening to John Denver, while yelling, "Whooo!" at pedestrians. Chuck wanted to ritualize my first kill by dipping his finger in the blood and wiping it on my face, but as he had done a poo in the forest, without access to hand-washing facilities, I told him that as a vegetarian this would not be appropriate.

Philadelphia

Made the long journey from Harrisonburg to Philadelphia for the sole purpose of visiting the famous Love Park. My girlfriend and I fought just hours before due to me stating that I would rather go see the Space Shuttle than visit her family, but apparently there is no Pissed Off at David Park. We then drove home during a blizzard using a TomTom GPS system stuck on bicycle mode.

The Space Shuttle

Prior to this trip, the only reason I had ever considered visiting the U.S. was because it has the Space Shuttle. Like a priest carrying home his first computer after hearing about child pornography on the Internet, I was practically foaming at the mouth in anticipation during the drive to the Smithsonian National Air & Space Museum. I have stood in front of masterpieces in art museums that did not raise an inkling of the emotion I felt upon seeing the space shuttle. It was at that moment I realized that the high horse on which I had laughed at Trekkies had sidled away in shame. On the way out, after spending the rest of our trip allowance at the museum shop buying plastic products made in China, I pulled my pants high up around my waist, gave my lunch money to a bigger boy, and considered going over to Windows®.

Belly messages
pretending to be a girl
on the Internet

Danni

. . . I will but first you have to write "I have a big Mr. Steve for D.T." on your stomach and e-mail a photo to me to prove you are genuine.

Hawk410

ok. Whats a Mr. Steve? A cock?

Danni

Sigh . . . yes Jamie.

Hawk410

Do you want my cock in the picture?

Danni

Just your stomach is fine.

Danni

. . . I would love to bounce up and down on you like a five year old on a jumping castle at a birthday party.

Scott_Mintred

Haha. id fuckn love that to. so are we gonna meet now?

Danni

Definitely but first write "I want you to bounce on me D.T." on your stomach, take a photo, then e-mail it to me to prove you are genuine.

Scott_Mintred

Cool.

Danni

. . . as I am very dirty and need somebody to lick my body all over.

Surfkilla

cool! I like dirty girls.

Danni

No, I mean literally dirty, the plumbing is broken and I have not showered in days. I will give you my phone number but first you have to write "I want to lick D.T.'s body all over" on your stomach, take a photo, then e-mail it to me to prove you are genuine.

Surfkilla

ok.

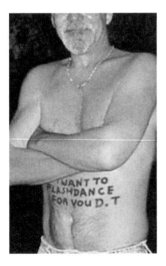

Danni

. . . we are actually only about five minutes drive from each other. Or in your case, a ten minute bus ride. You can call me but before I give you my number you have to write "I want to flashdance for you D.T." on your stomach, take a photo, then e-mail it to me to prove you are genuine.

Randbgeoff

What the fuck does that mean?

Danni

Um . . . flashdance means to ejaculate on someones chest I think.

Randbgeoff

Fuck ok. Sorry, I havent heard that one before. Hang on.

Danni

. . . yes, I have been very naughty. Will you spank me and tell me that I am a bad girl for spending my money on that Duran Duran record instead of buying you a fathers day present?

Southsidetom

Sure.

Danni

Ok but first write "I am your daddy D.T." on your stomach, take a photo, then e-mail it to me to prove you are genuine.

Southsidetom

No problem babe.

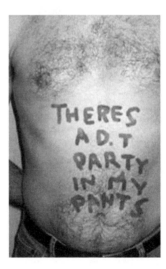

Danni

. . . yes but first you have to write "There's a D.T. party in my pants" on your stomach, take a photo, then e-mail it to me to prove you are genuine.

Romanticguy

What do you want me to write it with?

Danni

I dont care what you write it with, doesn't your wife have lipstick or something?

Romanticguy

All right.

Mr. Carganovsky
extreme stuntman to the max

....

Hello, my name is Mr. Carganovsky, and I'm Australia's most extreme stuntman to the awesomest max. If you have a party, wedding, or BBQ that you need a show for, contact me and I will do you a good price. I will soon be famous and the price will go up, so be quick.

....

I have been a professional stuntman for nearly four weeks, and in that time I have looked death in the face many times. My career began when someone clipped the side mirror of my Datsun 180B while I was parked at Kmart. I was inside purchasing credit for my phone at the time and did not notice the cracked mirror until I was driving home. A police car, with sirens blaring and lights flashing, came up behind me before overtaking, and due to re-fraction caused by the shattered mirror, I thought there were about forty police vehicles behind me and almost had an aneurysm. I have a few outstanding parking fines. I swerved, almost hitting a dog, before bringing the vehicle under control. The dog was on the other side of the road and behind a fence, but if it hadn't been, the outcome could have been very different. The adrenaline rush was unlike anything I had ever experienced, and the rest of the way home I drove sixty-three even though it was a sixty zone, as my need for speed had been fueled.

My most recent stunts include running on the concrete at my local swimming pool, putting aluminum foil in the microwave, and talking to strangers. This morning, while standing approximately three meters from a brick wall, I threw a golf ball at it as hard as I could. Due to the combination of physics and an internal rubber structure, it returned at almost the speed it left and struck me just above my ear on the right side of my head. I think

Stunt racks

Stunt visor

Stunt wipers

Stunt door

Stunt wheels

Stunt lights

I may have a concussion and cannot see in color. As such, I did not go to work today and instead spent the afternoon reorganizing my wardrobe, as I have way too many black and gray shirts.

To prepare for each stunt, I enter a deep meditative state through circular breathing exercises and twelve hours in my flotation tank listening to whale calls. As I do not own a tape of whale sounds, I make the noises myself. I am currently preparing for my latest stunt, in which I intend to play with pointy sticks, then eat and go swimming without waiting thirty minutes. Safety is paramount in the stunt business, so yesterday I bought a first aid kit for the glove compartment. The vehicle predates manufacturer requirements for air bags, but I have glued several rubber stress balls to my steering wheel and replaced the interior lining with bubble wrap. The car's exterior, engine, transmission, and tires are shot, but apart from that the vehicle is in excellent condition, so it is worth spending money on. Last week I had sign writers paint "Mr. Carganovsky, Exteme Stuntman to the Awesomest Max" on the side, and this has attracted a lot of attention.

Last night, I wrote and recorded my own theme song:

"Mr. Carganovsky to the Extreme"
By Mr. Carganovsky, music by Proclaimers

It's Mr. Carganovsky,
Being extreme to the awesomest max,
Did you see what he just he did?
No? Pity, because it was amazing.
Don't push him, because he is close to the edge,
Woh!

I am currently forced to bob my head and tap the steering wheel at traffic lights to disguise the fact I don't have a cassette player, so that people do not point and say, "Look, there's Mr. Carganovsky, sitting in his car in silence. He must be poor." Also, if I am touching metal when I turn the ignition key, I receive a short but painful shock, which often causes me to black out for an hour or two. This accounts for my being late to work at least three times a week, and I am on my last warning, but I don't care if I get sacked, as I will be famous soon.

With the money I make from being a famous stuntman, I am hoping to one day open a stunt school offering courses in flicking the light switch on and off repeatedly and sitting too close to the television.

RYAN
CARLISLE
THOMAS

LAWYERS

Level 3, 10 Queens Rd
Melbourne
Victoria
Australia
3004

Tel 1300 760 614
Fax (613) 8320 2906

Commercial law
Corporate law
Company structures
and restructures,
floats, mergers and
acquisitions and
joint ventures
Family law
Property law
Leases and rental
Taxation law
Wills
Liquidation law
Industrial relations
Insurance law

Mr David Thorne
PO Box 10476 Adelaide BC, South Australia 5000

Reference No. 003972THORNE

23.6.2009

Dear Mr Thorne,
I am writing to you on behalf of our client Skye Cargan. I
am under instruction to give you 48 hours in which to
remove all references to Mr Cargan from your website
27bslash6.com or we will begin legal proceedings against
you. Should you have any questions or response to this
request please call during office hours or email me at
craig.ellis███████████████████m.au

Sincerely,

Craig M. Ellison

Mr. Carganovsky's
lawyer writes a letter

From: David Thorne
Date: Friday 26 June 2009 11:02 a.m.
To: Craig Ellison
Subject: Skye Cargan

Dear Mr. Ellison,

Thank you for your letter. Does the forty-eight hours include sleeping time? I like to sleep in till around midday, often longer if it is cold and rainy outside. Today when I got up it was bitterly cold, so I sat on the couch watching *Blakes-7* DVDs wrapped in my comforter and, therefore, technically still in bed. If I bought two dunas, lay down on them with my arms and legs splayed out, drew the outline of my body, then cut out and stitched the dunas together to form a suit, I could wear this to the shops and even to work on cold days. People would probably look at me and say, "I wish I had one of those duna suits," and I would say, "Yes, it is very warm and comfortable and just like being in bed; therefore, I am exempt from any deadlines that may be placed on me."

Regards, David

From: Craig Ellison
Date: Friday 26 June 2009 12:55 p.m.
To: David Thorne
Subject: Re: Skye Cargan

Dear Mr. Thorne

The 48 hours includes sleeping time. I would advise you to take this matter seriously as anti harrassment laws are very specific and carry penalites ranging from fines to prison time. You would also be liable for all legal fees.

Sincerely, Craig Ellison

From: David Thorne
Date: Friday 26 June 2009 1:27 p.m.
To: Craig Ellison
Subject: Re: Re: Skye Cargan

Dear Mr. Ellison,

Does the forty hours begin from when you wrote the letter, when I received it, or when I chose to ignore it? Despite your inference, I do indeed take your threats very seriously. The thought of spending time in prison has caused my entire body to break out in a rash. It is a brown, even rash that makes me look as if I have been away on holidays and gotten a tan, so that is nice. While I am sure prison would have certain benefits, such as not having to decide what to wear each morning and the opportunity to meet new and interesting people, I have heard that they make you get up early and also expect you to shower in front of each other.

At home, I shower with the lights off, as I have a dim view of nudity. I also read once that the other prisoners make you dress up like a lady and dance for them, which does not sound like a safe idea. It has taken me years of practice to just walk in high heels, let alone dance. I would probably have to do one of those eighties dances where you just keep your legs still and dance with your arms and upper body, and the other prisoners would probably get bored and go and do other things. Unless I did the Robot, of course, which does not involve moving the feet much, and everyone loves the Robot. I know only two other dances: the Matrix, where you lean right back waving your arms slowly; and the old man dance, where I tense up, shuffle my feet intermittently, complain about the music volume, and sit down for a rest. I could probably tap dance as well, as it looks easy, but nobody likes that rubbish.

Regards, David

From: Craig Ellison
Date: Friday 26 June 2009 3:06 p.m.
To: David Thorne
Subject: Re: Re: Re: Skye Cargan

Dear Mr. Thorne

What does this all have to do with removing our clients name and photo from your website? I would strongly advise you not to ignore our letter. If references to our client are not removed by 5pm Wednesday 7th of July we will file a complaint with the courts pending instruction from Mr. Cargan.

Sincerely, Craig Ellison

From: David Thorne
Date: Friday 26 June 2009 4:21 p.m.
To: Craig Ellison
Subject: Re: Re: Re: Re: Skye Cargan

Dear Mr. Ellison,

I understand. In the event that this proceeds to court, will you appear for me as a character witness? I enjoy room temperature, pushing buttons with a really smooth push button action, and getting a little bit wet in the rain and then quickly running inside. Should you require more information, I am happy to meet up with you for a coffee or watch a DVD and discuss further. Have you seen the movie *Waterworld*? We could read to each other if you preferred. There is a chance we could even become close friends through this, which would be a nice outcome.

I read somewhere that lawyers are second only to dentists in regard to committing suicide, so you would have someone to talk to when you are down about everyone despising you. I would probably talk you out of committing suicide, and you would owe me your life and buy me nice things. I would pretend to feel uncomfortable about accepting them and say, "You don't have to feel obligated. That's what friends do," but really I would be quite happy about it. I am a size 32 in pants.

Regards, David

From: Craig Ellison
Date: Monday 29 June 2009 9:36 a.m.
To: David Thorne
Subject: Re: Re: Re: Re: Re: Skye Cargan

David, please just remove the references to Mr. Cargan from your website. He has not given you permission to use his image or name. His posting information on Facebook or Myspace does not make that information public property. I have spoken to Mr. Cargan in regards to this matter and while it is my understanding that he initiated the contact and the webpage was your response, it would be preferrable to all concerned that you end this now to avoid possible litigation.

Sincerely, Craig Ellison

From: David Thorne
Date: Monday 29 June 2009 10:09 a.m.
To: Craig Ellison
Subject: Re: Re: Re: Re: Re: Re: Skye Cargan

Dear Mr. Ellison,

I appreciate Mr. Cargan's preference for anonymity all too well. Each day before I leave the house, I dress as an elderly Jamaican woman and am well known in the community as Mrs. Cocowan. That way, if I ever find myself involved in a major crime, it is just a matter of time before they start looking for a large old black lady that sings for money at the train station and can run surprisingly fast. If I change Mr. Cargan's name would this be acceptable to you?

Regards, David

From: Craig Ellison
Date: Monday 29 June 2009 2:42 p.m.
To: David Thorne
Subject: Re: Re: Re: Re: Re: Re: Re: Skye Cargan

Dear Mr. Thorne

I have spoken to Mr. Cargan and we agree that changing Mr. Cargan's identity would be an acceptable outcome. I am glad we could bring this issue to an agreeable close.

Sincerely, Craig Ellison

That Tuesday
and why I was not at work

....

While my excuses for not attending work began as believable dental and doctor appointments, as the agency I worked for went from a thriving business with more than forty clients to trading while insolvent, I realized nobody cared if I was absent or what reasons I gave. As there were no clients when I did attend, I spent most of the day playing a game called "Staring at the wall wondering what happy people are doing" and answering calls while pretending I was a confused Cantonese woman. In a last-ditch effort to keep the few remaining clients we had, we invited them to join us at a charity dinner to buy musical instruments for starving children. The dinner started normally, with Thomas, the business owner, talking about his hair and a staff member leaving in tears after being accused of stealing, but went downhill from there. By the fifth Scotch, the entire table, including the managing director of McDonald's, sat in embarrassed silence as Thomas cried while telling a story about how, when he was twelve, his dog Trevor had died of testicular cancer. By Scotch ten, Thomas had vomited onto the leg of one client and perforated another's arm with a fork while flamboyantly telling a story about his experience in a Phuket brothel.

....

From: Shannon Walkley
Date: Wednesday 7 April 2010 9:02 a.m.
To: David Thorne
Subject: Tuesday

Hi. Where where you yesterday? Thomas tried ringing you.

From: David Thorne
Date: Wednesday 7 April 2010 10:47 a.m.
To: Shannon Walkley
Subject: Re: Tuesday

Dear Shannon,

I woke up late Tuesday morning. As a meeting had been planned for
9 a.m. with an angry client expecting a completed logo design four days
earlier, I realized the tune playing on my phone was not the alarm but the
fourth call from Thomas. Although fully intending to do the logo, I had
somehow instead spent the previous week on a knitting forum, under
the guise of "Edna," a seventy-eight-year-old woman with fourteen
grandchildren, making friends and exchanging tips before declaring that I
could "hear someone breaking in downstairs," then logging off forever,
giving them something more interesting to discuss than fractional
stitches and menopause.

Not caring as much as I probably should, due to working in an
industry devoid of conscience, I constructed a vaguely believable excuse
for being late in my head as I made a coffee, lit a cigarette, and turned on
the shower. Because of the age of the building, it usually takes around
five minutes for the water to heat, and I spent this time staring at the
shower curtain, which features the periodic table, wondering why I had
never heard of Seaborgium (106).

As I entered the shower and was soaking and lathering my hair with
shampoo, my phone rang for the fifth time. As I reached out of the
shower to answer it, I slipped, fell, and slammed my face, mouth first,
into the sink, knocking out two teeth and cracking another. Through the
pain, which was exactly like having my teeth knocked out with a
porcelain sink, I stemmed the blood with a Mr. Men T-shirt shoved into
my mouth while searching for a dentist online.

Confirming an emergency dentist appointment, I discovered the
clothes I had laid out, along with half the apartment, were spattered with
blood and my only other options were wet in the washing machine from
the night before. Figuring I would turn the car heater on high during the

drive, I pulled on wet trousers and a shirt, grabbed my phone, and locked the door behind me before realizing my keys were inside.

Kicking in a door is not as simple as action movies make it out to be, and my first attempt resulted in what felt like a sprained ankle. Hobbling to a side window, almost blind with pain and frustration, I picked up a potted aloe vera plant and threw it through the glass. Climbing into the apartment, now covered in blood and soil, I collected my keys and left.

After driving several blocks, I realized the dentist's address and phone number, written on my refrigerator door with a whiteboard marker, should have been reproduced onto a more transportable medium. Turning back, I arrived at the apartment to find two police officers at the premises responding to a report from a concerned neighbor about a possible break-in. Having established my identity and explained the smashed window, sprained ankle, wet clothing, missing teeth, and the blood and soil throughout the apartment, one of the officers stated, "You should probably go see a dentist."

I am not sure if it was my response to this statement or if they were just sticklers for the rules, but it was at this point I was issued a $235 fine for the four-inch potted marijuana seedling on my windowsill that I had received as a housewarming gift, despite pretending that I thought it was basil. As they left, one of them told me to "Have a nice day."

Taking a photo with my phone of the refrigerator door, I left the apartment. Halfway there, while on the phone to the dental surgery department, letting them know I was on my way, I heard a siren and looked in the rearview mirror to see a police vehicle with lights flashing. Pulling over and explaining why I was wet, limping, and had a Mr. Men T-shirt covered in blood held up to my face, I was issued a $218 fine for using a mobile phone while driving. The officer also pointed out that my vehicle was unregistered and had been so for fifteen days. Charged with such, I was informed that the vehicle would have to stay parked on the side of the road until I had paid the registration fees. As the vehicle registration office was only eight blocks from where my car was parked, I decided that walking there, despite my sprained ankle and gathering dark clouds, would be quicker than waiting for a taxi.

Arriving at the vehicle registration office almost an hour later, forced to rest several times, I joined a queue of approximately fifty people pretending not to notice the wet, limping, bleeding person with missing teeth. Calling the dentist to change my appointment to a later time, I caught a reflected glimpse of myself in a window. Due to the pain and loss of blood, my face was completely white, while the exertion of walking to the registration office had caused my mouth to bleed openly. I looked like a vampire. Not like the good looking one from *Twilight,* though—a limping, pissed off one. I realized I also still had shampoo in my hair. After what seemed like an hour of waiting in line, and was, I reached the counter and explained my situation to a lady so large her name tag was enveloped by a fold. Several minutes of one-finger typing later, possibly due to only one finger at a time fitting on the keyboard, she informed me that due to unpaid parking fines, I would not be able to register the vehicle until I had been to the courthouse and settled the $472.80 outstanding amount. Leaving the motor registration office, I had to duck and run from a bee.

While sitting in the taxi on the way to the courthouse, the bee, which I was sure I had eluded but must have been on my shirt, stung me on the inside of my left arm.

Arriving, I entered the building and joined the queue of approximately seventy other people there to pay fines. Surprisingly, I was not the only person there with missing teeth and blood on my face, and he gave me a knowing nod in what I assume was understanding or camaraderie. I felt like saying, "No, you have no fucking idea," but I simply nodded back, as he looked like the kind of person who might have a knife. Underestimating the waiting time, I called the dentist and changed the appointment again. After an hour of watching the area on my left arm where I had been stung grow to the size of a grapefruit and listening to the person in front of me yell at his girlfriend over the phone for kissing someone named Trevor, I reached the counter, paid the fines, and rang for a taxi to take me back to the motor registration office.

While I was waiting, an elderly man wearing a Salvation Army uniform asked me if I was all right and needed a place to stay, which I suppose was nice, but I was not in the mood for his crap at that moment and informed him of such.

Impatient after thirty minutes and no sign of the taxi, a bus pulled up, and I made a split decision to catch it. As I boarded the packed vehicle, I overheard a man tell his offspring not to stare. Explaining to the driver that not having caught a bus in thirty years meant I could not be expected to know about the exact fare rule or their inability to accept Visa, I paid ten dollars for the ride with no change. With the bus pulling away from the curb and turning down a street in the opposite direction of where I was headed, I jumped off at the next stop. Forgetting my sprained ankle, I landed awkwardly and fell. Having seen television shows where they tell you to turn a fall into a roll, the procedure was cut short by the bus stop pole. As I was pulling myself to my feet, the bus driver stepped off the bus and gave me back the ten dollars as the other passengers watched out the windows. As I waited for another taxi, it began to rain, causing the shampoo to run into my eyes. Swearing to never buy Schwarzkopf liquid pepper spray, a.k.a. shampoo, products again, I used the blood-soaked Mr. Men T-shirt to wipe the body of foam from my eyes and forehead.

Arriving back at the motor registration office, now with my left arm looking like Popeye's and the top section of my face painted red, I stood patiently in line for another thirty minutes, ignoring the stares and whispers, and playing "Delete everyone I hate this week from my phone."

After reaching the counter, paying the vehicle registration and attempting to call a taxi but finding my phone battery now flat from its previous lengthy exercise, I walked the eight blocks in the rain back to my vehicle to find a parking ticket for the amount of seventy-two dollars attached to the window and a missing side mirror, where someone driving past had hit it.

Finding the dentist office an hour and forty five minutes past closing time, I was informed that they would still see me but an after-hours emergency charge of $165 would be additional. As the dental surgeon was seeing another patient at a different clinic, I sat reading 2003 copies of *People* magazine for two and a half hours before he arrived. Apparently Ashton Kutcher and Demi Moore are dating.

Called in by the dentist, I asked for titanium alloy replacement teeth to enable me to chew through a porcelain sink in revenge, but neither of us thought it was very funny. Somehow during the surgery, possibly due to walking more kilometers that day than I had in the last ten years, I fell asleep while staring at a poster featuring a tube of Colgate toothpaste wearing an army uniform and shooting plaque with a machine gun. I awoke, as the dentist was finishing, with lips the size of armchair cushions but my teeth intact. As the process took more than three hours and involved an excessive number of large needles, stainless steel pins, and drilling, the invoice, including the emergency after-hours charge, came to $2,460.18 with another $58 prescription for painkillers and antibiotics.

I arrived home to find the apartment floor covered with a centimeter-deep mixture of blood, soil, and water, thanks to the rain coming through the smashed window; and my laptop, half my DVDs, and the television missing. Wading through to my bedroom, I climbed onto the bed, plugged my phone in, and fell asleep listening to messages from Thomas asking where I was and the fat lady at the motor registration office letting me know I had left my driver's license there.

Regards, David

From: Shannon Walkley
Date: Wednesday 7 April 2010 11:18 a.m.
To: David Thorne
Subject: Re: Re: Tuesday

Ok

Hello, my name is Jason,
and I own a MacBook Pro

Hello, my name is Jason, and I'm creative. I own a MacBook Pro. Do you own a MacBook Pro? It's OK if you don't own a MacBook Pro, because MacBook Pro's are for only creative people.

Everyone agrees with me that I am the most creative person they know. My MacBook Pro allows me to express my creativity by letting everyone know that I own a MacBook Pro. People sometimes ask, "Is that a MacBook Pro?" to which I reply, "Yes, it is. Because I am creative."

Once, when I was hiking and became lost in the wilderness, I was attacked by bears. Luckily, I had my MacBook Pro with me, which has my face as the desktop picture. I raised the screen high above my head, effectively looking taller to the bears, and they ran away. I then used the shiny titanium case to signal a rescue plane.

My Apple MacBook Pro

My MacBook Pro is the 12-inch 400 MHz version. People are stupid paying so much for the Intel Macs. I bought an iBook, painted it silver and used Letraset to write "MacBook Pro" on it. It is exactly the same as a real one, and as I use only Microsoft Word, it suits all my requirements.

Letter to Steve Jobs

Dear Steve,

Thank you for inventing the MacBook Pro. It is my friend and it is my lover. On the next model, could you please write the word "Pro" in bold?

P.S.: I watched Pirates of Silicon Valley *the other night and thought you were a bit mean to your girlfriend. Apart from that, you were really cool. I have a poster of you on my wall.*

Love Jason

The best thing about having a MacBook Pro is that you can take it anywhere. Now I can have Jason time anytime:

On the patio with a cold one.

Over a coffee.

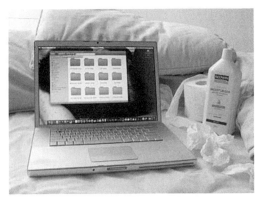

Curling up in bed.

Or just relaxing in the bath.

Tom the sad caveman

Write me a speech
and don't be a dickhead about it

....

When I was growing up, the only thing I wanted to be was an astronaut. This may seem like a normal aspiration for many children, but I was well into my teens, late teens, before realizing my chances were less than minimal. OK, mid twenties. The high grade requirements in physics and math may have something to do with it, but I prefer to blame the lack of space shuttle availability in Australia. I would have been a terrible NASA employee, anyway, preferring to spin around in capsules and jump high rather than spending my time connecting module bolt 962-A to 962-B. As an alternative to a career requiring high academic achievement, I chose one requiring none at all. A degree in design comprises mainly of taking copious amounts of drugs, wearing Doc Martins, and talking derisively about people who do not understand the difference between Helvetica Neue and Helvetica.

....

From: Thomas
Date: Wednesday 27 January 2010 3:12 p.m.
To: David Thorne
Subject: Speech

I have been asked to be part of the Speakers in Schools program this Friday and have to present a speech to the students at Bansia Park High School. It just has to be the opening speech and I will then go through the powerpoint presentation and show them examples of graphic design and branding we have done. I am very busy so can you write the opening speech? It just needs to be five minutes or so about the company and what we do. TJ

From: David Thorne
Date: Wednesday 27 January 2010 3:26 p.m.
To: Thomas
Subject: Re: Speech

Dear Thomas,

How does this affect your court order–imposed five-hundred-meter ban from schools?

Regards, David

From: Thomas
Date: Wednesday 27 January 2010 4:02 p.m.
To: David Thorne
Subject: Re: Re: Speech

Just write the opening speech please and don't be a dickhead about it.

From: David Thorne
Date: Wednesday 27 January 2010 5:16 p.m.
To: Thomas
Subject: Re: Re: Re: Speech

Dear Thomas,

I have attached the first draft of your opening speech. It may require a few tweaks but basically introduces you to the students and provides a clear understanding of what working in the design industry entails. Let me know of any changes you require:

Good morning students.
    My name is Thomas, and I have driven this extraordinary distance

from the nice suburbs to speak to you today despite the fact that I am not being paid to do so and it doesn't count as part of my community service. I had the secretary check. It has been a long time since I was in a school environment, and it brings back many memories—some fond, some painful. For many years I was called cruel names because of the size of my head, and rocks were thrown at me as I crossed the schoolyard due to being an easy target.

Thankfully, Mrs. Carter was eventually transferred to teach English at a different school, and the bullying stopped. It was obvious from the poor grade she gave me for my essay—about a space teacher who deals with racial issues when he transfers to a school on the planet Beta-5—titled "To sir, with the only emotional responses that can be generated by a species that has evolved in a methane atmosphere seventy times the pressure of Earth's," that her hostility masked a burning jealousy of my superior writing abilities, and I explained this to her on several occasions. A short time later, the replacement English teacher, Mr. Amorelli, asked me to stay back after class to discuss my grades but instead made me stand on a desk, undress slowly, and dance in a circular motion. At first I was afraid and ashamed, but then the power of dance overcame me, and I danced like I have never danced before. Like that welder in the movie *Flashdance.*

And that is what graphic design and branding is about. When the client asks you to fit eighteen pages of text onto a single-sided A4 flyer and increase the type size to twelve point, simply find your special place and dance. It doesn't matter if there is no music; create the rhythm by clapping, humming, or building a musical instrument using tightly drawn string and a cardboard box. A stick with bottle tops nailed to it does not count as a musical instrument. Nobody wants to hear that. I usually tap out "No Sleep Till Brooklyn," by the Beastie Boys, with spoons, but it comes down to personal preference and implement availability.

And here's a PowerPoint presentation . . .

From: Thomas
Date: Thursday 28 January 2010 10:02 a.m.
To: David Thorne
Subject: Re: Re: Re: Re: Speech

What the fuck is this? I told you not to be a dickead about it. Just write something normal that explains design and branding to young students please. I don't know how old they are probably 13 or 14. I have to present on Friday morning.

From: David Thorne
Date: Thursday 28 January 2010 10:38 a.m.
To: Thomas
Subject: Re: Re: Re: Re: Re: Speech

Dear Thomas,

I appreciate how important this speech is to you. It is entirely possible that in ten or twenty years these young students may be running their own corporation that requires design services and think to themselves, "Who was that man that came to our school and talked about his car, Discovery Channel, and his rooftop for four hours? The one with the large head. I should give him a call, because I need a business card designed."

I have, therefore, revised the speech accordingly to target this younger demographic. Let me know of any changes required:

Hello boys and girls. (Wave. With both hands so those at the back can see you.)

My name is Thomas, and I drove here in a motor car. Once upon a time, there was an evil wizard who tried to cast a spell on a young boy. Luckily, the young boy was able to defeat the evil wizard by doing a magical spinning dance. Without the use of bottle tops nailed to a stick. And that is what graphic design and branding is about: spinning really fast. (Demonstrate.)

And here's a PowerPoint presentation . . .

From: Thomas
Date: Thursday 28 January 2010 11:49 a.m.
To: David Thorne
Subject: Re: Re: Re: Re: Re: Re: Speech

I have to present this tomorrow morning. What the fuck is wrong with you? I will write it myself if you cant do as you are asked.

From: David Thorne
Date: Thursday 28 January 2010 12:26 p.m.
To: Thomas
Subject: Re: Re: Re: Re: Re: Re: Re: Speech

Dear Thomas,

All right, but going by the number of client proposals that have been sent out in the last six months, it has been a while since you have actually written anything. Just remember, the big letters mean you have started writing and the dots mean you have finished. The dots with tails mean you are talking, then pausing, then talking, and then pausing, again.

Regards, David

From: Thomas
Date: Thursday 28 January 2010 2:19 p.m.
To: David Thorne
Subject: Re: Re: Re: Re: Re: Re: Re: Re: Speech

The reason no client proposals have gone out lately is due to the global
financial crisis. My job is hard enough without you being a dickhead
when I ask you to write one fucking opening speech. For students! How
hard can that be? I have to give the speech tomorrow morning and I
expect you to e-mail me something usable before then.

From: David Thorne
Date: Thursday 28 January 2010 3:46 p.m.
To: Thomas
Subject: Re: Re: Re: Re: Re: Re: Re: Re: Re: Speech

Dear Thomas,

Thank you for explaining that the several hours of your day spent playing
online poker is a direct result of the weak U.S. dollar. I apologize for the
previous drafts, which I agree, with hindsight, do not give a clear
understanding of your important role. Please find attached the amended
and final draft:

Good morning students.

My name is Thomas, and I have been asked to speak to you today about
being a graphic designer and running a design and branding agency. I
never intended to be a graphic designer. I have always wanted to work
with cheese.

When I was a young boy I would make my own and go door to door
selling it in the small village where I was raised. One particularly warm
summer, I made enough money to buy a bicycle and started my own
home cheese delivery company, taking orders via two-way radio. I

painted a pair of my father's overalls bright yellow, cutting holes to symbolize Swiss cheese, and rode throughout the village calling, "Cheese! Cheese for sale!" People would often point and say, "There's that kid on the bicycle who makes his own cheese. Look at the size of his head." Eventually my business was shut down due to government officials not understanding the self-fermentation benefits of guinea-pig milk, but not before I learned the benefits of company branding and had raised enough capital to start my own branding company.

Unfortunately, my design director David Thorne, who has been responsible for the majority of high-profile client branding projects for the company over the last eight years, just formally tendered his resignation, effective immediately. David cited the inability of the company owner to actively seek new clients, a salary that professional bag ladies would ridicule, third-world working conditions, and beating his own high score in an office game he devised called "Staring at the wall, wondering what happy people are doing," as his main reasons.

David thanked the staff and me for the opportunities that were provided to him during his time with the company and wished me all the best with my personal and professional endeavors. And with the speech.

And here's a PowerPoint presentation . . .

From: Thomas
Date: Thursday 28 January 2010 4:13 p.m.
To: David Thorne
Subject: Re: Re: Re: Re: Re: Re: Re: Re: Re: Re: Speech

Fine.

From: David Thorne
Date: Thursday 28 January 2010 4:26 p.m.
To: Thomas
Subject: Re: Re: Re: Re: Re: Re: Re: Re: Re: Re: Re: Speech

Fine.

Dear Jason
a guide to fine art scanning

....

Hello, my name is Jason. I'm often asked about fine art scanning, so I have compiled this handy guide to building your own equipment. I discovered fine art scanning when I was about twelve or thirteen. Around 97 percent of people, male and female, scan fine art regularly, and it is a healthy and normal exercise. Those that do not are usually suffering mental or physical problems, so it seems strange that fine art scanning is still seen as taboo or embarrassing these days, and the term "fine art scanner" derogatory. In actuality, the term "non-fine art scanner" should be more insulting, as it hints at a mental illness. Those that are required to scan fine art should be encouraged and commended on such a socially responsible activity.

....

Q. Dear Jason, sometimes I scan fine art when I am at work. Is this normal, or should I see someone about it? Thanks, Chris.

A. Scanning fine art at work is completely normal, Chris. I am currently scanning fine art as I write this. My favorite place to scan fine art is in public places, such as movie theaters and playgrounds. Sometimes when I scan fine art I like to imagine I am on stage or speaking at a conference.

Q. Dear Jason, sometimes I think about firemen when I am scanning fine art. Is this normal? Rob.

A. It is perfectly normal, Rob. I often imagine I am a fireman or army man when I am scanning fine art.

Q. Dear Jason, I have heard that scanning fine art too much can cause blindness. Is this true, or did someone make that up? Cheers, Mike.

A. Hello Mike, I can honestly say there is no truth to this rumor. I regularly scan fine art thirty to forty times a day with no negative results. Once, during back-to-back episodes of *Gilmore Girls*, I scanned fine art one hundred and twelve times with no adverse effects.

Q. *Dear Jason, I am left handed and I was wondering if this will affect my ability to scan fine art effectively. Best, Steve.*

A. Being left-handed is an advantage, Steve; I myself am right-handed but use my left, leaving my mouse-hand free.

Step 1
Take one roll of Oreo cookies out of the packet.

Step 2
Cut off the end of the packet and remove the cookies.

Step 3

Roll the end of the packet over several times until you have a smooth, rounded bevel.

Step 4

Choose a photo of someone you would like to scan fine art with. Place the packet bevel over the lips and trace around the circumference.

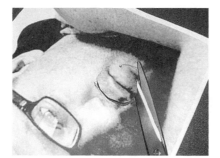

Step 5

Cut out the area you have drawn. Remember to cut inside of the line to ensure the right size.

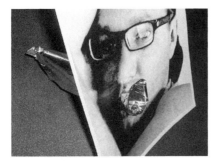

Step 6

Insert the packet into the hole you have just cut until the bevel is flush with the picture.

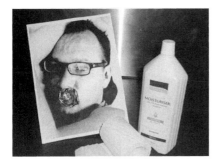

Step 7

And there you are. Your home-made fine art scanning device is complete.

Scott
Dunning-Kruger effect poster boy

When not appearing as poster boy for the Dunning-Kruger effect, Scott divides his time between eating and "writing" on his beige blog, attempting to prove to the world that everything I write is fake.

From: Scott Redmond
Date: Friday 17 September 2010 2:11 p.m.
To: David Thorne
Subject: Fake

Davey Davey Davey. You let the ball slip on this one. Your article about George from West Virginia calling you a foggot must be fake because you are in Australia which is 13 hours and 30 minutes ahead of West Virginia. Seeing as you would use your local time in your e-mails, this would mean George would be awake and writing e-mails at 5:21am, 8:38am, 11:48pm, and 1:32am unless you have a time machine.

Scott

From: David Thorne
Date: Friday 17 September 2010 2:44 p.m.
To: Scott Redmond
Subject: Re: Fake

Dear Scott,

Thank you for sharing the results of your time zone research. While some might describe your behavior as obsessive, I prefer to think of you as special. Like one of those children that spins until they vomit or collects Pogs. Despite having nobody to play Pogs with. Although I am currently in the U.S., rendering your blunt point less pointy, I do, coincidentally, own a time machine.

My time machine is shaped like a closet. I discovered its capabilities purely by accident one day when I climbed in, sat there for a bit, and emerged to find myself in the future. Which is almost exactly like the present except a little darker. I was expecting to see robots and flying cars, but there weren't any. If I had a flying car, I would fly to your house and say, "Look, Scott, I have a flying car; I would love to take you for a ride, but unfortunately, your weight exceeds that of future antigravity propulsion technologies." You would probably become irrational with envy and attempt to catch me, but due to what few leg muscles you have, atrophied from too many hours spent on the computer researching world time zones, you wouldn't be able to jump very high, and I would hover just a few inches above your sausage-like finger flailing.

While I have not yet been successful in my attempts to travel backward in time, only forward, if I climb into the closet backward, this will probably work. I plan on traveling back to the year 2009 to see what it was like before continuing my journey back to your grade seven class and explaining to a young Scott Mintred that while his current metabolism may be able to cope with forty Twinkies per day and an exercise routine consisting of breathing and blinking, it is patently going to catch up with him later in life. I will also attempt to explain that time spent on obsessive jealousy is time that would be better spent exploring his own capabilities. I will then give him a slap.

I have attached a drawing of my time machine should you wish to build your own in order to travel back several hours to construct a better argument, or several years, to take up jogging.

Regards, David

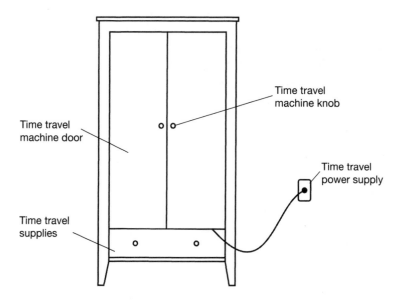

Time travel machine knob

Time travel machine door

Time travel power supply

Time travel supplies

From: Scott Redmond
Date: Friday 17 September 2010 4:27 p.m.
To: David Thorne
Subject: Re: Re: Fake

Lolcats5000. Your nonsense and lies prove nothing. I'm easily twice as intelligent as you are, I'm not fat and at least the stories on my blog are factual. Should it make for less interesting reading, then so be it. You should do some research on time travel before you make a fool of yourself. To travel through time you need to travel faster than the speed of light. A closet can't move. If I built a time machine I'd do the world a favor and go back in time and stop your mother from reproducing.

Scott

From: David Thorne
Date: Friday 17 September 2010 5:12 p.m.
To: Scott Redmond
Subject: Re: Re: Re: Fake

Dear Scott,

Your attempt to convince my mother not to procreate would be unsuccessful, as I would simply go back a few minutes before you appeared and tell her not to listen to men wearing elastic waistband pants. I would also hide behind a tree until you showed up and give you a slap as you waddled past.

While it would be irresponsible for me to condone your obsessive behavior, I do understand it. When I was in grade three, I was obsessed with a girl named Emma Jenkins. As neither of us knew cursive, I sought to impress her by tracing several pages of script from an old manuscript and, stating that it was a love letter and I had known cursive since the age of two, presented it to her. That night, Emma's father rang my mother with instructions that I was not to communicate with their seven-year-old daughter again. Either socially, or via letters describing her child-bearing hips and round Victorian buttocks. Another time, obsessively jealous of the fact Bradley McPherson had been selected to play the lead role in our fifth-grade school play, I constructed a plan to make him ill. Figuring this would automatically give me his role of King of the Faeiries and someone else would take over mine as tree number two, I collected several snot-laden tissues from my flu-ridden sister's bedside table and took them to school the next day. With a thin film of the mucus covering my hands, I demonstrated to Bradley the correct procedure for shaking hands before betting him that he could not fit a whole fist in his mouth. Unfortunately, while Bradley was fine the night of the play, I was not. Unable to find a replacement for tree number two and dosed up with half a bottle of Robitussin and several flu tablets, I managed to fulfill my role of standing still with my arms held up for about ten minutes before inexplicably deciding it would be appropriate to sing "The Safety Dance," by Men Without Hats. Luckily, Emma, dressed as a giant mushroom, broke my fall as I passed out.

Although, going by your argument, you have just e-mailed me at 2:57 a.m., meaning your e-mail must be fabricated, I accept your critical analysis of my design and have attached a modified version incorporating your technical and personal requirements.

Regards, David

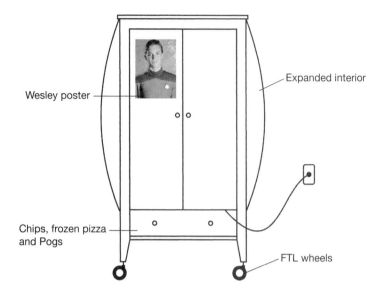

Wesley poster

Expanded interior

Chips, frozen pizza and Pogs

FTL wheels

From: Scott Redmond
Date: Friday 17 September 2010 5:31 p.m.
To: David Thorne
Subject: Re: Re: Re: Re: Fake

I don't like Wesley jackass and you really aren't the sharpest knife in the drawer are you, if I told your mother not to reproduce you wouldn't exist to go back and talk to her. Coup de grace.

From: David Thorne
Date: Friday 17 September 2010 5:40 p.m.
To: Scott Redmond
Subject: Re: Re: Re: Re: Re: Fake

Dear Scott,

If you had managed to persuade my mother not to procreate, I would not exist to send you the plans for constructing your own time machine in which to travel back in time to persuade my mother not to procreate. Apparently, this is known as a pair of ducks. I have no idea why but assume it alludes to the fact that if a duck were capable of constructing a time machine and traveling back in time to meet itself, there would be two of them. One would probably need to wear a hat or something to avoid confusion. If I did go back in time and meet myself, I would have a good look at the back of my head. If you went back in time and met yourself, you would have someone to play Pogs with.

From: Scott Redmond
Date: Friday 17 September 2010 6:12 p.m.
To: David Thorne
Subject: Re: Re: Re: Re: Re: Re: Fake

I'd go back in time and punch you in the back of your head.

From: David Thorne
Date: Friday 17 September 2010 6:15 p.m.
To: Scott Redmond
Subject: Re: Re: Re: Re: Re: Re: Re: Fake

Dear Scott,

I would travel back five seconds prior to you doing so and tell myself to duck.

Regards, David

From: Scott Redmond
Date: Friday 17 September 2010 6:27 p.m.
To: David Thorne
Subject: Re: Re: Re: Re: Re: Re: Re: Re: Fake

I'd just go back 5 seconds before that and punch you in the back of your head before you tell the other you to duck.

From: David Thorne
Date: Friday 17 September 2010 6:34 p.m.
To: Scott Redmond
Subject: Re: Re: Re: Re: Re: Re: Re: Re: Re: Fake

Dear Scott,

I would travel back five seconds prior to that and tell both my other selves to duck. Perhaps that is where the term "pair of ducks" originated.

Regards, David

From: Scott Redmond
Date: Friday 17 September 2010 6:48 p.m.
To: David Thorne
Subject: Re: Re: Re: Re: Re: Re: Re: Re: Re: Re: Fake

It's paradox imbecile, not pair of ducks. For someone who thinks they are smart you are not very smart. My intellect is far superior to yours so it would be simple for me to stay one step ahead of you. Just as I always do. I'd just go back and stab you before you were born or go back to 1998 and register the name google and use some of my billions to pay for a hit on you.

From: David Thorne
Date: Friday 17 September 2010 7:22 p.m.
To: Scott Redmond
Subject: Re: Re: Re: Re: Re: Re: Re: Re: Re: Re: Re: Fake

Dear Scott,

As no man is an island, regardless of size, it is hardly surprising that the weight of your obsession would require hiring professional help. But your attempt to purchase the Google name would prove unsuccessful, since I would travel back to 1988 and invent the Internet, adding a clause that Benny Hill look-a-likes with pathological disorders stemming from issues with self-confidence and self-esteem, are not allowed to use it.

This would not only foil your plan to own Google but also save people the misfortune of clicking on your blog when googling the word "beige." Although encouragement, rather than reprimand, may be the key to persuading a slow child to stop defecating in the bath, there eventually comes a time when you just pull the plug and slap him.

Regards, David

From: Scott Redmond
Date: Friday 17 September 2010 8:36 p.m.
To: David Thorne
Subject: Re: Re: Re: Re: Re: Re: Re: Re: Re: Re: Re: Re: Fake

My website isnt beige imbecile. Its a color I invented called Priceless Coral. It looks a lot better than your artsy-fartsy nonsense and is a lot better designed. Learn from someone that knows what they're doing on the internets. Good design is about readability and great content. I'm not interested in continuing this converstation when I have already proven my point so you can fuck off now.

From: David Thorne
Date: Wednesday 13 February 2019 12:03
To: Scott Redmond
Subject: Message from the future

Dear Scott,

This is David from the future and I am sending you good news. Due to changes in media-based stereotypes, spherical is now considered the ideal body type and Pogs is an Olympic sport. Also, priceless coral is the new black.

Regards, David

From: Scott Redmond
Date: Friday 17 September 2010 9:12 p.m.
To: David Thorne
Subject: Re: Message from the future

I said fuck off imbecile. Don't contact me again and if you post any of my e-mails you will have a legal suite.

From: Scott Redmond
Date: Thursday 16 September 2010 8:02 p.m.
To: Scott Redmond
Subject: Proof that David's stuff is fake

Dear Scott,

This is Scott from the past, and I am sending you good news. It seems
David has let the ball slip. His last article about george from West Virginia
calling him a foggot is obviously fake because he is in Australia which is
13 hours and 30 minutes ahead of West Virginia. Seeing as he would use
his local time in his e-mails, this would mean George would be awake
and writing e-mails at 5:21 a.m., 8:38 a.m., 11:48 p.m., and 1:32 a.m.
unless he too has a time machine. You should e-mail him this fact.

Also, you are awesome and girls think you are hot.

Scott

Hello, my name is John,
and I ride a bicycle

My bicycle has a titanium composite alloy such as NASA uses on the space shuttle, and it has Shimano gears, which are the best. People often say to me, "That's a nice bicycle, John," and I reply, "Yes, it is made out of a titanium composite alloy such as NASA uses on the space shuttle, and it has Shimano gears, which are the best."

Every day, I ride my bicycle to the local cafe to meet other people who ride bicycles, and we drink coffee and talk about bicycles.

Riding a bicycle has many advantages. As you do not have to register bicycles or obey any road rules, I am currently constructing a four-person family bicycle that consists of two bicycles welded together with four armchairs in between. Due to the extra weight, I have added an engine and am devising a roof, doors, and storage area at the back, allowing us to ride in all weather conditions and take it shopping.

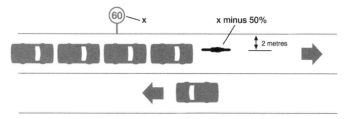

Correct bicycling speed and position.

Sometimes when I am riding my bicycle I feel like I am the only person on the road. If I have my earphones in and the iPod turned up really loud, I cannot hear the car horns and people yelling, "Get off the fucking road!"

Little compares to the exhilaration of listening to Queen's "Bicycle" while riding in the center of a lane at half the speed limit with several hundred cars banked up behind me during peak hour traffic. Riding a bicycle is also an excellent way to quickly go downhill.

I am often asked why my Spandex® bicycle riding costume features eight hundred and thirty corporate sponsorship logos even though I do not actually have a sponsor. The reason for this is simple. For every thirty male bicycle riders, there is one female bicycle rider and, as in nature, where the most adorned peacock gets the peahen, the male bicycle rider with the most brightly colored Spandex® and most corporate sponsorship logos gets to mate with her.

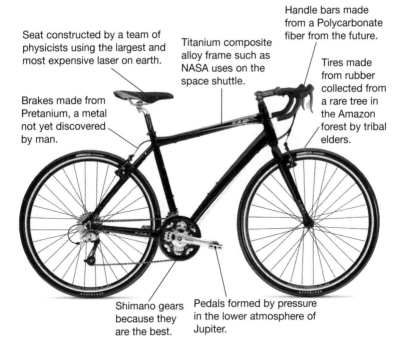

Handle bars made from a Polycarbonate fiber from the future.

Seat constructed by a team of physicists using the largest and most expensive laser on earth.

Titanium composite alloy frame such as NASA uses on the space shuttle.

Tires made from rubber collected from a rare tree in the Amazon forest by tribal elders.

Brakes made from Pretanium, a metal not yet discovered by man.

Shimano gears because they are the best.

Pedals formed by pressure in the lower atmosphere of Jupiter.

Road safety is an important component, and basic precaution needs to be undertaken. Once when I was riding my bicycle at great speed, I developed speed wobble and was thrown, rolling several times and sliding several meters, toward a busy intersection. I was lucky enough not to enter the flow of traffic thanks only to friction. As bicycles do not come with safety airbags, I now carry an inflatable raft and pump with me at all times. A lot of people choose not to ride a bicycle because they are too embarrassed to wear a crash helmet, but by painting the helmet light brown, it can easily be disguised as a large mushroom.

Things that are almost as good as riding my bicycle:

1. Looking at my bicycle
2. Talking about my bicycle
3. Watching television programs that feature people riding bicycles
4. Cheese

Hello, my name is Josh,
and I live in New Zealand

....

New Zealand is the most beautiful country in the whole world, and one day I will be king of it, because my mum says that people with red hair are descended from royalty.

....

I live in Wellington, the capital of New Zealand. It is the best village in the whole world and a thriving metropolis with seventy-four residents. When I grow up I want to drive the village car. My plan is to drive to the neighboring village in the middle of the night and steal their fire. The residents of Wellington will probably build a mud statue in my honor like they did for my uncle Robert when he caught a pig.

Every day I play the national sport of "throw a stick," where you throw a stick. It is so much fun, and often I will spend the entire day throwing a stick. Each night when I climb into bed, I practice by throwing twigs across the room in preparation for the next day's game of throw a stick. When I am not playing throw a stick, I play a game called "Find where the stick went."

My auntie, who is also my second cousin and the village prostitute, pays me two shells, the New Zealand currency, to sit on her porch and watch out for uncle Robert. I have a lot of shells, and I keep them on the beach. My uncle Robert—who is also my nephew, the official village pig catcher, and head of New Zealand tourism (famous for the catch phrase: "At least it's not Adelaide")—has initiated several projects aimed at increasing tourism to New Zealand. These include an annual four-day "Look at the Sheep" festival, sheep rides, a "famous sheep through history" exhibition, and a guided tour in the village car to view local highlights such as sheep.

If I were a sheep, I would write something in the dirt with a stick, becoming famous and the subject of much scientific and media interest. I would be rich and buy a Porsche.

Every seventy-four days, when it is my turn to wear the village shoes, I go hiking through the sheep paddocks, enjoying the feeling of not having sheep droppings between my toes, then climb a hill to sit at the top, singing. My favorite song is called "Kahadanhibrakahana," which, roughly translated from Maori, means "I am sitting on a hill." As I share a bedroom with seventeen siblings, this solitude is something I look forward to. Sometimes I play throw a stick, but usually I just masturbate.

Bees are attracted to yellow— it is a scientific fact

....

A few months back, while I was meant to be working, I filled out a company's online contact form by instead listing my household furniture and asking what they would give me for it all as trade-in on a R 1200 GS motorcycle. Several years ago, I did some work for a guy named Andrew, who drove to work in a brand-new, bright yellow convertible one day. I think it was a Renault. I told him that it is a scientific fact that bees are attracted to yellow. Being highly allergic to bees, he then refused to drive with the top down, claiming that bees did actually seem to congregate around his car. He would not even drive with the windows down. I think the bees may have simply smelled his fear and approached out of curiosity, as I had made the scientific fact up. I also sold him a computer, stating that it had twice the amount of megatron as other available systems.

....

From: Peter Conner
Date: Friday 9 Jan 2009 9:17 a.m.
To: David Thorne
Subject: R 1200 GS

Hello David,

Thank you for your recent enquiry regarding pricing of the R 1200 GS Motorcycle. We do not accept household furniture as trade ins on

vehicles and would reccomend you sell them privately. The R 1200 GS
has a list price of $25,470. Please note that this excludes Dealer delivery
and ORC and is GST inclusive. I welcome you to contact me personally
to arrange a test ride at a time that would suit you.

Sincerely, Peter Conner

From: David Thorne
Date: Friday 9 Jan 2009 10:03 a.m.
To: Peter Conner
Subject: Re: R 1200 GS

Dear Peter,

Thank you for responding to the online request I filled out several months
ago and your kind offer to allow me to test ride the product before paying
what is essentially five times the value of my car. If you could confirm
for me that the model is available in desert yellow, I would be very
interested.

Regards, David

From: Peter Conner
Date: Friday 9 Jan 2009 10:22 a.m.
To: David Thorne
Subject: R 1200 GS colors available

Hello David,

Yes the R 1200 GS is available in desert yellow. We have a desert yellow demo model on the showroom floor at the moment if you would like to come in to view and arrange a test ride at that time.

Sincerely, Peter Conner

From: David Thorne
Date: Friday 9 Jan 2009 10:48 a.m.
To: Peter Conner
Subject: Re: R 1200 GS colors available

Dear Peter,

I have just been informed that bees are attracted to yellow vehicles. Apparently, a few years back, a guy I know purchased a bright yellow convertible and was unable to drive it with the top down due to constantly being surrounded by bees. Do you know if this is a scientific fact? I am allergic to bees, and the last thing I want is to be stung in the eye while I am doing 240 kilometers per hour on the freeway during the test ride. Also, do you know if there are airtight motorcycle helmets available?

Regards, David

From: Peter Conner
Date: Friday 9 Jan 2009 11:09 a.m.
To: David Thorne
Subject: Re: Re: R 1200 GS colors available

Hello David,

You would be required to follow state speed restrictions of 100kph on the Eastern Freeway during a test ride and would reccomend lower speeds than that until you have familiarized yourself with the bike. We would generally not expect people to take the demo bike on the freeway but we can discuss when you come in. I have never heard that about bees liking yellow vehicles and would think it is not true. The R 1200 GS is available in granite, black and red in addition to the yellow. Would you like to come in today and discus?

Sincerely, Peter Conner

From: David Thorne
Date: Friday 9 Jan 2009 2:50 p.m.
To: Peter Conner
Subject: Re: Re: Re: R 1200 GS colors available

Dear Peter,

I have been researching bees on the Internet for the last four hours at work. When I type "Do bees like yellow?" into Google, it states that there are 2,960,000 results. It will take me a while to look at that many pages, so I doubt I will make it in there today. One of the pages states that Qantas once had a yellow kangaroo as their logo, but when it was painted on the tail fin it attracted nests of bees, so the logo was changed to red in the mid fifties. This would seem to support the argument that bees are indeed attracted to yellow and contradicts what you have told me. Admittedly, though, another page states that bees are technically unable to fly due to their wings being too small for their body weight, but I have seen them doing it, so this can't be true—somebody should check the Internet and make sure everything on there is correct. Regardless, I do not think having to dodge bees in addition to the already present dangers of learning to ride a motorbike for the first time would be very safe. Once when I was a passenger in a yellow taxi, a bee flew in and I screamed, causing the driver to swerve and hit a wheelie bin. I will continue my research and confirm that this would not be a factor before I arrange the test ride.

Regards, David

From: Peter Conner
Date: Friday 9 Jan 2009 3:18 p.m.
To: David Thorne
Subject: Re: Re: Re: Re: R 1200 GS colors available

When you say you are learning to ride a motorcycle, do you hold a current full motorcycle license?

Sincerely, Peter Conner

From: David Thorne
Date: Friday 9 Jan 2009 3:40 p.m.
To: Peter Conner
Subject: Re: Re: Re: Re: Re: R 1200 GS colors available

Dear Peter,

No, but how hard can it be? They are just pushbikes with engines. Part of my daily job role is to ride to collect coworkers' lunch orders from McDonald's. I balance the bags on my handlebars because they will not buy me a basket. I think that qualifies me for something. Often, I have to make the trip twice when McDonald's® employees leave something out of the order. Actually, on average, every third time I go through the drive-through, they forget to include part of my order. Also the girls who work there are too attractive. This means that if I want something from my local McDonald's® late at night, I have to shower, shave, and wear something nice before I can get a simple snack. As it takes me at least two hours to do my hair, I am practically starving by this time and therefore order twice as much food as usual. Ordering more food increases the chance of them leaving something out. Last night it was an apple pie, and that is really the only thing I like from there. It is quite obvious to me that they do this on purpose.

Once, I ordered two Big Macs (minus the beef), large fries, and an apple pie. When I got home and opened the bag, there were two happy meals in there. The toy in each was a Kim Possible figurine, which worked out well, as I gave one to my son and kept one myself. For a cartoon character, you have to admit that Kim Possible is quite attractive. I also have a thing for Lois from the television series *Family Guy,* so I must have a penchant for cartoon redheads, which is vaguely puzzling to me as I cannot stand redheads in real life. Nobody can. I read somewhere that redheads are more prone to allergies, and if this is a scientific fact, and includes allergies to bee stings, all redheads should be encouraged to wear bright yellow T-shirts.

Regards, David

From: Peter Conner
Date: Friday 9 Jan 2009 4:28 p.m.
To: David Thorne
Subject: R 1200 GS test ride

Dear David,

I apologize but we will be unable to organize a test ride for you at
this time.

Sincerely, Peter Conner

Barnesyfan67
online dating profile

Hello, my name is Joanne. My favorite pastime is practicing laughing in the mirror, but I also practice dancing so as to be prepared in case I am out and someone puts "Bat Out of Hell," by Meat Loaf, on the stereo. I also have all the Fleetwood Mac concerts on VHS and have practiced until I have all of Stevie Nicks's moves down pat. I dance for my mother sometimes. I was raised by my two mothers in a large commune whose ideologies included balance with nature, meditation, and weaving dolls out of straw. When I was nine I was traded to wandering gypsies for six onions. I graduated primary school in my late teens from School of the Air. As we did not own a CB radio, I took all my lessons by tapping Morse code onto nearby electrical wires. I have a poster of a dolphin in my bedroom and have a picture of a tiger on my quilt. I call the tiger Mishka. Sometimes I lie on my quilt and pat him and tell him about my problems. I enjoy sitting in my favorite chair at the window.

My Ideal Partner

I would like to try one with hair this time. It doesn't matter if they don't have all their teeth, I don't either—LOL. My last boyfriend, Darren, had a wicked sound system in his Commodore, which was awesome, so that would be good. My Datsun has an Audio 4 system that kicks. It has an input plug so that you can play your songs on your iPod through it, which is great. I don't own an iPod but if I had a friend with an iPod and they wanted me to drive them somewhere, I would be like, "Hey, girlfriend, let's play your music on your iPod through my stereo. Do you have a N33 adapter cable?" and they would have one, and we would listen to Keith Urban on the way to Target.

My Ideal Date
Probably something normal, like Friday night line dancing at the local pub after a nice meal—either McDonald's or Barnacles Bills. I don't mind; I enjoy both red meat and seafood.

Location
I live really close to the train stop, which means I can catch the train to the bus stop that takes me to the tram that takes me to a suburb near the city. Which is really handy because, if I knew someone else who lived close to the city, we would always be meeting in the city to shop for clothes, drink coffee, and talk about Cold Chisel. I have a mobile phone tower in my backyard.

Best Holiday
I'm saving up to go to Bali. Bali is a beautiful and spiritual place, and accommodation is very cheap because a lot of villagers drowned to death. Once when I was six, my legal guardians took me to the beach, and while I was wading, the crab-covered corpse of a cruise ship entertainer named Julian washed up on the beach. I hope one of the dead villagers doesn't wash up on the beach while I am relaxing in Bali. Thousands were washed out, but I would think that they would have been eaten by crabs and sharks by now, which is quite beautiful and spiritual when you think about it. Darren and I used to go crabbing.

Favorite Music
Cold Chisel. I love every album and every song ever released by the Chisels. The Chiz! The depth and, dare I say it, the poetry in Jimmy's musical

storytelling leaves me breathless. If Jimmy Barnes knew how much I truly understood what he was telling me, he would know that he has found his soul mate, and he would get on his Harley Davidson motorcycle and come to my place, and we would be lovers. Sometimes when Jimmy is singing, it is like he is talking only to me. My favorite is the track that goes "Kay San, you don't have to put on the red light." If we were on a beach together we would hold hands and spin in circles and laugh like children. If I couldn't marry Jimmy, I would marry Keith Urban and raise wheat on his farm together. Sometimes he would play his guitar, and I would sing while I whittled wood.

Favorite Movies

The greatest movie ever made in all time is *Pretty Woman*. Many people do not get the symbolism in the movie because Julia Roberts did not play her role very well. Sometimes I practice conversations in the mirror, and I was in a play once so I would have been much better than her, and the relationship between me and Richard Gere would have been more honest and believable to the viewer. The second-best movie ever made is *Top Gun*. If I had to pick a third-best movie ever made, I would have to call it a tie between *The Blues Brothers* and *Dirty Dancing*.

Favorite Books

I don't read books, but I did once listen to a book on tape called *Flowers in the Attic,* by Virginia Andrews. It was great and reminded me a lot of my own life. Listening to a book on tape is like watching television with the brightness turned down and everyone talking in the same voice but is the whole book in 180 minutes, which saves a lot of time. Watching television is heaps better. I own a Teac television because they are the best. My ex-boyfriend Darren bought it for me from Cash Converters. It was ninety dollars, but he talked them down to seventy-five and got two VHS videos with it—*Splash* and *Cannonball Run.*

Favorite Television Shows

My favorite show ever was *The Young Ones* on channel 2, and I have styled my hair based on the character Neil. Other shows I love are *Australian Idol* and *Rove*. *Rove* is so funny. I like it when he does other people's voices. He was a crab in the movie *Finding Nemo,* did you know? It was so sad how his girlfriend died. I once had a boyfriend who I thought died, but it turned out he had moved to another suburb with his new girlfriend and thought it would be easier if I was told he had been in a forest fire. *Friends* is also a great show; everyone on there is just like the friends I would have.

My Poetry

"My Gaping Soul" *By Joanne*

The sadness and the joy are one. The sadness is a cold, frightened mouse. The joy, a song of life. Like the Bon Jovi song where he is at the Grand Canyon.

"Always Being There" *By Joanne*

When my boyfriend Darren was working, I would ring him every hour to tell him I loved him. I would visit him at his office bi-hourly. True love is always being there. Why did he have to rescue those children from that forest fire?

"My Chair" *By Joanne*

My chair is near the window. Every day I sit in it. I have Venetian blinds, so I can see out but people can't see in. If I turn the lights out, I can sit there the whole night and nobody knows I am watching.

"Ruffles and Others" *By Joanne*

I have a cat named Ruffles. I have more cats, but they are referred to as "others," as I cannot think of eighteen names.

"Choices" *By Joanne*

The photos on the neon-backed menu boards at McDonald's never look like the actual product. Except the apple pie. I will have one of those.

Sponsor a poor black boy

....

He stinks and ate a rat with maggots today.
How would you like it?

....

Bababada Didva *Poor black boy*

SEND
MONEY
NOW!

Lesley
the adventurous, outdoors type

Having received a love letter from Lesley in regard to the page about the poor black boy, I had a quick glance through his personal website. The website, written by Lesley, about Lesley, and featuring several photos of Lesley, describes Lesley as ". . . the adventurous outdoors type with a love of watersports and everything outdoors." Wasps are outdoors Lesley, do you love wasps? Fuse boxes? Open cut mining? Pedestrian crossings?

Things that people have e-mailed me that are outdoors and therefore Lesley loves:

Traffic lights, Prickles, Litter, A bus, My sister Amanda, Flies, Cigarette butts, Land mines, Homeless people, Sticks, Grandma, Dark alleyways, Bins, Opera in the park, Feral cats, Playgrounds, Dust, Used condoms, Fat people at hot dog stands, Blowfish, Construction workers, Snipers, Shade, Airborne viruses, Mandy Says toilets, A box, Shoes because of the carpet, Wading pools, Children on a field trip, AstroTurf, Lesley, Indians on public transport, Holes in fences, Tether ball, Starving third-world children, My poodle Benny, Quicksand, Lawn sausages, For Sale signs, Boy Scouts, Peeping Toms, Lawn furniture, Flagpoles, Television antenna's, Owl pellets, Street walkers, Forest fires, Techno Viking, Public toilets, Yellow snow, Speed bumps, Lost kittens, Free candy vans, Cement, Garden gnomes . . .

From: Les Copeland
Date: Thursday 15 Jan 2009 4:19 p.m.
To: David Thorne
Subject: Poor black boy

What kind of a complete fucking moron makes fun of starving children?
What a pathetic attempt at humor. I have spent time in third world
countries and seen children starving with my own eyes and I think you
seriously need to grow the fuck up.

Les

From: David Thorne
Date: Thursday 15 Jan 2009 6:41 p.m.
To: Les Copeland
Subject: Re: Poor black boy

Dear Lesley,

Thank you for your kind e-mail. I am glad you enjoyed the website. In
answer to your question, no I cannot send you a photo of myself without
a shirt on. I have, however, attached this photo of a mouse riding on a
toad's back. It is a visual metaphor for how you must have felt writing
that last e-mail: magnanimous, the world on your shoulders, and moist.

Regards, David

From: Les Copeland
Date: Friday 16 Jan 2009 10:28 a.m.
To: David Thorne
Subject: Re: Re: Poor black boy

Are you fucking retarted? Where did I ask for a photo of you? I wrote to you about the poor black boy page. As If I would want a photo of someone who thinks starving children are funny. You need a punch in the head. And my name isnt Lesley moron. Tell me where you live and we will see how fucking funny you are.

Les

From: David Thorne
Date: Friday 16 Jan 2009 11:02 a.m.
To: Les Copeland
Subject: Re: Re: Re: Poor black boy

Dear Lesbian,

Thank you for your request, but I regret that I am unable to provide you with an address, as I am homeless. Please send money and/or Legos. I have been collecting Lego blocks for nearly four years now, since I intend to build my own home. I currently have exactly 1,692,008 blocks of various sizes and need only another 4,836,029 to complete my plans of constructing a four-bedroom home with sunken lounge and indoor pool. Prior plans to build a home from seawater were abandoned due to physics. The advantages of using Lego blocks over traditional materials, in regard to durability and gaiety, are without question. The only issue is finding a block of land with a flat, green plastic base. Gaining council approval shouldn't prove to be an obstacle, as my local member of parliament, Kate Ellis, is known for her stance on environmentally responsible architecture and is a close friend. Although we are yet to meet, I send her several e-mails each day and often stand outside her house. As her front door is more than ten meters from the sidewalk, this does not violate my court order. I have attached a photo of Kate Ellis as a sexy space girl in case you do not know who she is.

Regards, David

From: Les Copeland
Date: Saturday 17 Jan 2009 2:09 p.m.
To: David Thorne
Subject: Re: Re: Re: Re: Poor black boy

I have no idea who the fuck that is and it wouldnt suprise me if you were homeless loser. spending your time writing shit like that instead of getting a real job like a grown up what are you 15? Did your mummy buy you the computer you are using? Why dont you turn off your computer and go outdoors there is a whole world out there. and Les is short for Lester moron. I seriously want to punch you in the fucking face.

From: David Thorne
Date: Saturday 17 Jan 2009 2:37 p.m.
To: Les Copeland
Subject: Re: Re: Re: Re: Re: Poor black boy

Dear moLester,

I appreciate the suggestion but dislike the outdoors; it has bees and sharp sticks in it. Once, when I went camping with my sister, she became angry at a comment I made regarding her girth and drove off leaving me stranded two hundred and thirty kilometers from the nearest McDonald's. By the third day I tried eating grass, and chased a small lizard on the fourth. If you and I had known each other then, you could have arranged an emergency UNICEF food-parcel drop. As it was, I survived only by making love to keep warm and building a vehicle out of my clothing, which enabled me to reach the nearest town, where I danced for food.

You and I should go camping together sometime, as you seem like an adventurous, outdoors kind of guy with a love of water sports and everything outdoors. I read somewhere about a father and son who went camping and during the night a tree branch fell on their tent, killing the child, so I always sleep the farthest distance possible from my son when we are camping together. Safety first. You would be a handy person to have along in case we became lost, because we could use your Village People mustache as kindling to create a signal fire and your naturally reflective surface to alert search planes.

In regard to getting a real job, my current position as assistant to the managing assistant in charge of envelopes fills much of my spare time, and I have been promised a promotion to assistant to the assistant manager in charge of assistants within ten years. The corporate stepladder has my name on every rung. Also, I understand your need to assert yourself physically—I too can experience true intimacy only through pain. As I have ventured onto your website and seen your photo, my only requirement would be that we keep the lights off because imagination has its limits. I have had worse, of course, my last girlfriend was the poster girl for "Love is blind," and my current partner is overseas at the moment, so the only intimacy in my life involves a stick of salami and the neighbor's dog when Glenda and Frank go out Tuesday nights.

Once when they arrived home early due to an argument between them regarding Frank's Internet usage, I hid in their wardrobe for four days. As I could see Frank using his computer from my hiding position, I can vouch for his denials to Glenda's accusations that he was "looking at girls on the Internet." He was looking at photos of her. No, not really. It was men.

To prime myself for your proximity, I have printed your photo out and have it sitting on the couch next to me while we watch a DVD together. Occasionally, I throw an M&M at you and pretend you giggle and tell me to stop it. We are watching *Nanny McPhee,* which always makes me cry. The bit at the end where her wedding dress materializes out of snow is simply beautiful, but my favorite scene is where the robots turn on their human masters.

Regards, David

From: Les Copeland
Date: Saturday 17 Jan 2009 6:41 p.m.
To: David Thorne
Subject: Re: Re: Re: Re: Re: Re: Poor black boy

You are a complete idiot. Dont e-mail me again.

From: David Thorne
Date: Saturday 17 Jan 2009 6:57 p.m.
To: Les Copeland
Subject: Re: Re: Re: Re: Re: Re: Re: Poor black boy

OK.

From: Les Copeland
Date: Saturday 17 Jan 2009 7:02 p.m.
To: David Thorne
Subject: Re: Re: Re: Re: Re: Re: Re: Re: Poor black boy

Fuck off

About the author of 27b/6

David Thorne works in the design and branding industry as design director for a small Adelaide design agency because he is too lazy and easily distracted to do a real job. Among his multitude of qualities, which include reciting prime numbers backward from 909,526, reading to blind children, and training guide dogs, embellishment may be at the top.

David currently lives with his partner (who recently made the top 100 on *So You Think You Can Dance*) in the small country village of Adelaide, which is commonly referred to as the murder capital of Australia. This title is given to Adelaide not due to the volume of murders, but due to the clever antics of Adelaide's finest serial killers. Ironically, Adelaide is the only Australian capital city not founded by convicts. He was born in Geraldton, Western Australia, to Welsh immigrant parents and has one sibling, an older sister, who once attempted to set his bedroom alight with him locked inside. Police did not press charges.

He has worked as a horse-riding instructor, bartender, Macintosh design system consultant, graphic designer, copy writer, branding consultant, and design director. Describing working in the design industry as "the most uncreative experience of my life," he began writing articles for his website as a distraction from spending each day making the type-size larger on clients' business cards, assuring his boss that his hair looks nice, and making rubbish look appealing so that people will be tricked into buying it.

David reads too much, generally exceeds others' tolerances, and likes Linkin Park. He stays up too late, drinks too much coffee, smokes too much, hates getting up in the morning, and has offspring who think David doesn't know what he has been up to when he deletes his Internet history.